Craig Grimes
The Aching Lust For Crime
(Revised Edition)
978-1-895166-54-5
Printed and bound in North America.
2025. Insignificant Diversions
New Brunswick, Canada
Originally published in 2013
by Charivari Press

THE ACHING LUST FOR CRIME

(REVISED EDITION)

CRAIG GRIMES

People,
a fallen people,
dead-of-heart, dazed and lonely,
beneath the sinister burden of their own corpses,
wandered from exile to exile,
the aching lust for crime sweltering in their hands.

– Farugh Farrokhzad, *Earthly Verses*

...in a time that is both long ago and today, both waking and dreaming, both reality and illusion...

1.

Sunday: bodies falling from the heavens

Keith Shadwell, as he did most nights, was standing in the dark, at the window of apartment 708 with his right hand resting on the waist high sill and staring out through the night. He was watching a woman in the apartment building directly across the road. She was reading. He would often watch her for hours while she read.

Oh, wait, she pulled her legs up under herself. Keith's hand gripped the sill more tightly.

Keith was a parasite on others' lives. It was as if he was a void, an absence needing something to fill him up. His face was triangular with large ears and pointed nose that together gave him the appearance of a possum. This might be a fitting metaphor for his character: nocturnal, solitary, and fraudulent.

The word solitary didn't strictly apply however. He had little contact with the outside world but he did periodically sleep with a woman who lived on the third floor. They arranged get-togethers through notes pushed under their front doors; notes with little meaningful content beyond establishing a time and place. They were meaningless nothings. Not so sweet nothings, like *Much Ado About Nothing*, where love is invoked by whispered nonsense.

Keith never used the woman's name – which was Ida – and it might well be that he'd forgotten it.

He abruptly jumped back when some indefinable dark matter plummeted past his window. Stumbling against a chair he gripped its back for support. The projectile outside was indiscernible as anything but a blurry mass, yet human nature had recognized impending death and instinctively recoiled.

Keith did not approach the window and look down. Instead, he turned his face towards a nearby bookshelf crammed full of books about criminals. His comfort place. There were books of every type: biographies, histories, novels, photography. He preferred the true crime mags from the forties and fifties with their heady mix of crime and porn.

"You wanna be a mobster, don't you?" Ida had once asked.

5

"I was born at the wrong time," said Keith, then qualified the comment by adding, "It's actually just that I find those who live secret lives interesting," which didn't dispel the notion that he sympathized with the criminals and not the police.

"Everyone's real life is secret," she answered. "It's called self-preservation. Especially for the misfits and maligned."

There was no sound on the seventh floor when the lump struck the pavement below but a scream soon confirmed it was a body. This was followed by yelling, barely audible to Keith.

He turned his face back towards the window. His expression was now serene, as if bodies falling from the heavens required no more empathy than that expended on heavy rain; just something to be greeted without undue concern because the inconvenience would soon pass.

After staring impassively for a moment, Keith left his apartment and rode the elevator to the first floor where shaken tenants with lowered voices were beginning to congregate in the lobby, in front of the mailboxes.

Several residents were also clustered outdoors, moving in and out of the pools of orange light beneath the faux gas lamps beside the front entrance. The face of the corpse (laying off to one side) was covered by what looked to be a green, haphazardly strewn sweater, a puddle of blood seeping from under it. The nearby group stood with their backs to the body and blood, their heads held high, looking up the street toward the approaching sirens.

Inside, in response to a whispered question from Keith, an older man said that the victim lived in apartment 1308. Voices murmured assent and another man added how the deceased was a 'nice kid' who was new to the building and lived alone.

"It's gotta be suicide," a woman contributed.

"You never know. He coulda been thrown from his balcony," a sensationalist offered, "what with all the gangs in the area. You see the type hangin' round."

"Jesus," someone blurted, clearly shocked.

"Oh yeah," said another in a knowing way.

Heads nodded. A cabal of conspiracy theorists was

6

forming.

"Poor boy," muttered an old lady and the mounting energy subsided in shame.

Keith stared in evident fascination at the speaker who had introduced the idea of the mob being responsible for the human downpour, but instead of furthering that conversation his next comment was a non sequitur.

"I was looking out the window just as that guy was going by. Our eyes locked for a split second. You know? It was weird, I've never seen a more intense yet tranquil look."

The tenants gaped at Keith, obviously impressed with his invented story of mystical communion. It would get passed around in the days to come; easily the most impressive story regarding the death of the kid. (During that same period, Keith would avoid the front entrance to the building, and when he eventually resumed using it, would invariably stare upwards and frown as if surveying for impending human precipitation.)

He spun around and extracted himself from the group, without comment, as if suddenly remembering something, then walked to the elevator and rode it to the thirteenth floor. Turning right on exiting, he followed the ashamed and dingy grey-carpeted hall around a corner to apartment 1308, glanced back over his shoulder, and tried the door. It was unlocked and he entered.

Keith flicked on the overhead light and looked about at an apartment clearly disabused of any pretense of dignity. There was a mound of dirty clothes beside the couch (a crumpled sheet on it suggesting that this was where the tenant had slept). He closed the apartment door behind himself, feeling self conscious about his mounting arousal. This was better than the crime mags; this intimate look into the secret world of someone's possibly criminal life.

Keith tentatively advanced to the bedroom, empty except for an open suitcase in the middle of the floor. He turned and began to wander about. There was no dining table or chairs. No bookshelf. No books. The balcony door was propped open to the night, framing a rectangle of black void.

Keith reached down to the coffee table that was covered

with empty pizza boxes and take-out containers, and snatched up a black baseball cap with a yellow Mac's Trucking crest stitched to the front. As he ran his fingers over the crest, he felt the surge of forbidden excitement from the tactile experience, and he shivered.

Keith put the cap on his head. Catching his reflection on the TV screen, he turned his head left and right, assessingly, and smiled his approval.

Bending over again, this time to reach for something on the floor, he lurched forward, apparently vertiginous from the movement of blood to his head, and stumbled against a small end table. It and a lamp went over on their sides with Keith futilely waving at them.

"Son of a bitch," he swore. Reaching down to pick up the table and lamp, balance restored, he heard a faint chime signalling the arrival of the elevator on the thirteenth floor.

Keith scuttled across the apartment, shoved open the front door, fled down the hall, and slipped into the stairwell.

When the police and the building superintendent turned the corner of the hall they froze at sight of the open door to 1308.

"Stay here," said one of the officers to the superintendent, while reaching out his arm like a locked turnstile. He put a hand over his gun (his partner followed suit) and they slowly moved forward.

They peeked around the door.

"Hello. Anyone here?" the first officer called nervously before moving into the living room.

His partner sang the same tune while moving past him to check out the bedroom, and soon announced an all clear.

The cop in the living room glanced about, scrutinizing. "Looks like there was a fight."

"The balcony door's open," added his partner.

A meaningful look was exchanged.

"Oh my God, what a mess," said the superintendent, her face peeping around the front door of the apartment, "and he was always so neat, except for that ratty ball cap he always wore."

"Ma'am," said the bedroom cop. "Please wait in the hall

8

and don't touch anything else."

Detective Rose, who arrived on the scene moments later, would write in his report: 'There is a lack of furniture and care for hygiene which suggests the apartment may have been retained with a short term in mind'. He didn't mention the Mac's Trucking cap, now missing, although the building superintendent had twice advised him of the fact. Rose thought the hat was inconsequential although it had apparently always been attached to the deceased's head and didn't appear to have gone over the balcony with it.

2.

Monday: a keen, intuitive understanding of the metaphysics of a knife in the back

Louis was a smallish, thin guy in his late forties who claimed (i.e. possibly lied) to have once high fived Brian Mulroney in an airport (although he had nothing but contempt for the man) and occasionally read the poetry of Alexander Pope. He could 'recite' some Pope, partly from memory and partly from the lack of it:

> *Let us (since Life can little more supply*
> *Than just to look about us and die)*
> *Expatiate free o'er all this scene of Man;*
> *A mighty maze! but not without a plan;*
> *A Wild, where weeds and flow'rs promiscuous shoot,*
> *Or Garden...*
> [something, something, something]
> *...of man.*

Joseph, his nineteen-year-old travelling companion, had no interests beyond watching television in the lounge area of the psych ward and laughing raucously at any political news, which caused people lacking in English language skills to assume they were missing something. In fact, they merely lacked the ability to appreciate the absurd. Joseph had a delicate and sweet face.

Together, the two were walking through a motel parking lot on their way to breakfast.

"I should write this as a short story someday," said Louis, about the events he was relating. "Cus like I said, it has symbolic value." The phrase 'symbolic value' was uttered with extreme gravity, plunking down on every syllable, declaring this to be something of profound significance.

The events, as Louis described them, had happened many years before. He'd gone to a woman's house to retrieve some stuff for her, after she'd left her boyfriend. The guy had dumped everything on the lawn.

"He's heaved it down on the ground, you know? Think about it, the shape of the stuff means it's met with some violence from him. In my story I'd want to make that clear, so he becomes representative of unhinged violent capability, the thinness of civilization, you know? The veneer of...of...he's a threat. So I don't know what to do. This psycho looks like he wants to kill me. I figure I should just go and forget taking anything – that seems to be the rational thing to do – but I'm ascared that as soon as I turn my back on him he'll pounce. So I freeze. Like I'm paralyzed by the potential for violence, wishin' I had a gun. So I'd end the story there. Do you see how it shapes up? The dilemma? It's a summary of modern life, right? Vulnerability in the face of barely controlled psychotic power. An inability to move because of the threat of violence."

Joseph's look said that he saw no such thing, but he nodded gravely despite a pretty strong feeling that Louie was full of shit.

The two men passed through the front doors of the motel and into the lobby.

Louis had brightened when telling his story, stepping away from the dark emotional cloud he'd been under that morning after awakening and realizing 'they' were nearby. He hadn't needed to see them, he just knew. He prided himself on always having had a keen, intuitive understanding of the metaphysics of a knife in the back.

Louis and Joseph slowed as they walked down the hallway that led to the dining room, allowing two screamingly macho wannabes, with blocky frames and shaved bullet heads, who'd come through the lobby doors after them, to draw close.

Louis, looking back over his shoulder, said to the men in an urgent voice, "We need to talk. There's a room up ahead."

Together, the four proceeded in two-by-two lockstep with the determination and purpose of a military drill. The newcomers kept well behind Louis and Joseph, and away from each other, as if getting too close to another man was a sign of failing to be sufficiently manly.

The larger of the two men was Charlie, and the smaller man – older and more surly – was Sonny.

The four men soon came to a stop in front of the dining room doors, each of them surveying the diners through a bank of windows.

"In here," Louis said, pointing to an empty meeting room across the hall, before leading the way in.

Charlie and Sonny followed.

Joseph got as far as the meeting room doorway and took up a position there, as if he was a guard. He had something else on his mind however. He was watching a busgirl in the dining room who he'd caught sight of. She was staring back. She bumped into a cart of dirty dishes and flushed.

Louis took a seat at one of the meeting room tables and Charlie sat across from him.

Sonny, the attention seeking sort who always makes a pronouncement on entering a room to announce their presence, jumped his butt up onto a second table causing the thing to scrape across the floor, screaming in protest. Sonny beamed with pride at his accomplishment.

"So what's up?" Charlie asked Louis.

"They're nearby," Louis began.

Sonny jumped up off his table and said, "Fuck!"

"We gotta get away and change our identities, now, before they show up," continued Louis calmly. "Get somewhere far away and change our names."

"Yeah, for sure, get the fuck outta here," chimed in Charlie, loud and decisively.

"We should change our last names to the same thing," Louis said brightly, with obvious hopeful intent, his tone making it clear that this was a plea and not just an idea being thrown out for consideration. "We can all go live in the same trailer park, somewhere in Florida; say we're brothers. Nice eh?" He chuckled and added, "Gulfstream's open all year." He grinned, as if that would shape a positive emotional response to his ridiculous scheme.

"Naw, I don't think that's a good idea," said Sonny in a slow paternal manner. "Me and Charlie bin talkin' 'bout what'll happen if they show and figured we'd get out fast and go in different directions."

"'s right. 's the best way," Charlie affirmed, looking at

12

Louis. "You're on your own. We all are. We're outta here!"

With that he stood up and strode from the meeting room with the calculated disdain of a baseball umpire turning his back on an ejected player.

Joseph stepped smartly out of the way.

Sonny followed his partner and together they retreated whence they'd come, down the hall, quickly, while remaining vigilant about maintaining the bullet head's requisite distance between men.

"Don't worry," Louis said kindly to his young friend, as he stepped into the hallway. He turned his head to watch the retreating figures.

Joseph, slouched against the doorframe, not appearing to be nervous in the least. He briefly smiled indulgently at Louis before his attention turned back towards the dining room and the busgirl.

Louis sighed, watching the retreating bullet heads, but quickly disconnected himself from them and snapped to attention. He turned to Joseph, followed that one's gaze, and said, "So ya ready to eat?"

"Yeah." Joseph grinned back.

"Daydream number 7a?"

"7b."

"Ah. Don't go too far with that, eh."

Louis liked to talk about what Joseph was thinking and feeling. The two had met in a psychiatric unit, so it was natural to introduce a degree of openness about what they were thinking into their friendship. 7b, as far as Louis remembered, was a romantic fantasy where, in a very rapid period of time, Joseph would imagine first meeting the object of his attention, then daydream in great detail about some key stopovers along the route of the developing relationship – marriage, children, trials and tribulations – until eventually settling into a long meditation over where the two would retire.

The problem with the 7's – a, b and c – was that, at some point, once old age had set in (in the daydream that is) Joseph would begin contemplating his own death. The scene, as he imagined it, was usually so touching and vivid that he would

13

begin to cry and manifest signs of severe and self-destructive depression. It was important that Louis keep on top of what his young companion was fantasizing about to help him maintain equilibrium.

Forty-five minutes later, Louis and Joseph sat on a park bench on the edge of the motel lawn. In front of them were twelve metres of beach, and beyond that, the lake. Louis held a piece of toast in his hand.

"You figure they gonna head back to Calder Racetrack?" asked Joseph, referring to the departed men.

"This time a year? Naw, Saratoga."

"Like the hoi polloi."

"Yeah. It's the season of summer leisure. And for those two there's nothin' like chasin' the great American Dream of beatin' the odds and gettin' money you didn't earn."

"Is that what they mean when people talk about the 'American Dream'?"

"Depends. It ain't the version they tell you, 'bout hard work and makin' a success of your life that way. Pullin' yourself up by the bootstraps. That's just a line rich people use to keep you workin' for them. It's the carrot on a stick. For some other people I know, like Frick and Frack there, the American Dream's about beating the system: by getting rich with no work, like the way most billionaires got that way – by getting money from Daddy. I once heard 'bout a guy bought a two dollar win ticket when he was teaching a college course on horse racing economics. It was a winning ticket but instead of cashin' it the guy had it framed and hung on the wall as some sort of educational prop that he could use in his course. He got fired at some point after that. Seven years later he broke into the college, stole the ticket and cashed it. It was the principle of the thing. A winning ticket needs cashin', even if its only worth a dollar more than it cost. For both sorts of American dreamers, you can never have enough money. It's a compulsion."

Joseph laughed loudly before saying, "So you're goin' to chase it: the American Dream?"

Louis shrugged. "It's not my type of dream. You can't

14

chase my sort. It's a bit like the original pre-American dream; goin' way back. To escape to a new land. With freedom to think what you want. And gettin' by with little money; with just what you can get on the odd exacta at the track. My dream doesn't depend on anyone else, or finding luxury. I do haveta get some money together to start though, of course. A few bucks to buy my Mayflower. I'd like to get an old van and win enough to put up in a campground for the season. No more boondockin' and living in Walmart parking lots for awhile."

The two of them settled into calm complacency, considering busgirls and horse racing respectively, and looking out at the lake.

Intermittent gusts of wind caused undulations of the willow branches above them, while below on the ground, dappled shadows pooled and puddled. Birds trilled love songs and broke hearts while others wailed melancholy dirges. A few seagulls and geese wandered the sand and grass, feigning disinterest, birds of business with weighty matters on their mind, until Louis flicked the last bit of his toast to the ground. Something like thirty angry street tough birds suddenly appeared from nowhere to wrestle over it, switchblades out, all pretence of cool detachment gone.

"So how do you know they're nearby?" Joseph asked.

"Can't say. Just woke up this morning and knew."

Joseph nodded, satisfied, although who 'they' were had never been explained to him, despite his asking. He had parsed Louis's comments for clues, and he'd entertained multiple possibilities of who 'they' might be – the mob, cops, fans, bullies, political enemies, women, doctors – it was always something new so he couldn't be sure. Louis's two recently departed friends seemed to assume that he was saying it was the cops who were closing in. He and his two pals had obviously been up to something, Joseph thought, before Louis had swung by the hospital to pick him up a few days earlier.

"Don't know what it is," Louis continued, "but I've just always had this thing, like a sixth sense, same as if it was a wild animal watching me in the bush; you just all of a sudden know it's there. That there's eyes on you. But I'm sorta lookin' for it too. The past is always followin' me in one way or another."

"What's that mean?"

"Lately, it's more and more my memories. All the things I ever did won't leave me alone. Things I said. Stuff I didn't think to do. Stuff I did do. Bad choices. Wrong ones. They pile up the older you get, and when there's less of the hustle and bustle and bull-headedness of life you have more time to think back. I understand why old people long to die sometimes. They wanna escape from memory. They say death is crossing a river that washes away memories. It's the only way to really escape. Only death can end memory."

Joseph looked out over the undulating waves washing up on the shore, constantly erasing its contours, washing clean its memory of the shoreline. His expression said that he was clearly disturbed by the speech, despite an innate ability to grasp something that was mostly just self-indulgent bullshit. He eventually formulated a pained response. "You shouldn't wanna die. You're only forty-six."

"Memory is awful. It leads to regret," Louis said clinically, "even about little stuff." He easily sported this cold detachment because he wasn't the one affected by his pose, but in fairness, he did experience pain, and that pain was life itself. He'd developed a cowardice with respect to life and often said he regretted not being able to take the approach of Alexander Pope who used to carry two loaded guns and his Great Dane with him to avoid attacks. But it was the masked assassins called memories that Louis now feared most. And how do you defend yourself against those? Oh, if there was only a switch to turn your head off.

"But you can't live without memory," protested Joseph. "Without memory you can't even find your way home. Maybe you just gotta take the good with the bad. I can think of some bad shit I did but there's nothing I can do about it so I let it go."

"Yeah, that's true enough, memory is part of life, but that's the problem: you can't get away from it and it can really start to get to you. There's only one way out."

16

Joseph looked desperate at this insistence on the merits of death. Louis was the only thing he had left. "My grandfather was in a lot of pain when he died and he struggled to live…"

"So, you're saying I'm being self-indulgent? That life has value? Yeah, maybe."

Joseph didn't answer, unsure if that's what he was saying. Silence ensued. "I'm gonna pack," he said finally, rising.

"Hm."

Joseph left. He knew the routine.

Louis remained, soon becoming absorbed with a horde of ants engaged in their labour with the protestant work ethic he lacked. Some crawled across his feet. One, who started up his pant leg, was batted away.

Eventually Louis got up and began in the direction of the door to his motel room. He walked beside a public pier that snaked adjacent to an inlet running up to the motel. The pier and the public beach on the opposite side of the inlet were becoming crowded with residents of the nearby town who jammed them every Sunday, their cars lining both sides of the road in each direction, as far as you could see. Suddenly Joseph was beside him, gripping his arm.

"We haveta go," Joseph said.

"I gotta take a leak," Louis answered.

"There's no time. They're here, in the hotel!"

"I'm just goin' to our room."

"You can't. There's two men went in there. It's time to leave. Our stuff's in the car."

The pair walked along the dock and past the motel. The curtains rustled in their room when they went by it but no one looked out.

Joseph noticed an empty police car in the motel parking lot but didn't waste his time speculating about whether the men in their room were connected to it or if they were the 'they' that Louis had sensed were chasing him.

Joseph and Louis climbed into their stolen purple Capri – whose glove compartment had fortunately contained a wallet with a credit card in it that they'd used to cover their motel room – drove out of the parking lot, and headed east.

17

3.

the million humiliations

The foreman, Billy Lisle, somewhere in his early forties, sported a brown outfit he referred to as 'my uniform', composed of stock items from Mark's Work Wearhouse that he imagined gave him the social status of a skilled tradesman like his father.

He'd had his name stitched onto the shirt because – like many people who have nothing going for them, whether they're a bum or a president – he wanted to convince people that he was something he wasn't: a star at what he did. Billy was going places. He had the ticket.

Billy sat atop the conference table in the meeting room with his back to Ida. His feet were on the seat of a chair and he looked through a window towards the factory floor, studying three elderly Asian women working on adjacent machines. Each would periodically raise her head and say something to the other two that made them all laugh. It only made Billy angry. He hated old Asian women.

He clasped a clipboard, holding Ida's resume, on which he'd scribbled a couple of notes.

Ida wore a blue clingy dress for the occasion – the one that seemed to generate an animal response in Keith – and sat in a chair on the other side of the table. She was nearing forty, had watched the Olivier version of *Wuthering Heights* seventeen times, and thought that Keith was appealing because of his 'brooding' silences. His personality seemed to be cold, but Ida felt this was just a protective cover, and anyway, she had learned not to expect too much from men who, more than once, had described her as 'trailer'. She now often thought of herself, and of what she deserved from life, in that way.

Ida was sitting beside her friend Sally. They'd been shown into the room together, even though Sally's interview was supposed to follow Ida's.

When the foreman had first entered the room, and immediately begun the interview without asking Sally to leave, Ida had puzzled over his lack of professionalism. She was shocked when he next turned his back on her, and parked his butt on the table, but quickly decided that this behaviour made sense if the interview was only a formality; the positions as good as theirs. This was just as well since it was hard to smile and act enthused about dull questions when the job confirmed the death of your dreams.

The two women were best friends and had been looking for work since the plastic company had laid them off. This was their chance, they said, to finally get out and find well-paying jobs that would afford them the Caribbean cruises and ski trips they'd always fantasized about taking some day. It was those daydreams that had kept them going into work on the shittiest days at The Plastic Man, the worst being those in mid-summer where they struggled for breath because of the combined heat from outside and from the machines unrelentingly spewing plastic bottles. The closing of the factory was a blessing, they told themselves. But after dozens of fruitless applications, Ida and Sally were now back to looking for the crummiest sort of crummy factory job; the only kind that either had ever had.

Billy Lisle's utterances were punctuated by distracted breaks, his attention teetering on the edge of an abyss, fascinated with the women outside the room. "So you were (pause) there ah, oh (pause) at, ah, where was it (scanning the resume), The Plastic Man for ah, fifteen years?"

"Nineteen." It was the second time the question had been asked and answered.

"What? You said fifteen before." The tone was accusatory.

Ida hadn't – and her dates of employment were listed on the resume that Billy had on his clipboard – but she said, "Oh, sorry," just the same.

Billy frowned as he spun around after only four questions. When he looked up, his eyes immediately went to Sally, sitting there; a picture of innocence. He grinned stupidly.

For fuck's sake, thought Ida.

"Okay thanks," Billy said, turning to Ida, his smile gone as he removed her resume from his clipboard and lobbed it onto the table.

Ida stared at it, feeling the contempt of the gesture.

19

"So tell me about yourself," said Billy, looking down at Sally's resume. "Sally," he read aloud before she could answer, dragging out the word very slowly, an obscene molestation of the naked syllables. "I see you also worked at The Plastic Man." He smiled his most impressive tradesman's smile.

"Seventeen years."

"Seventeen! Wow!"

"Give me an example of your initiative," he said, and followed that with, "What's your strongest quality?" then, "What's your weakest?" The banality of the questions belied the presumption of Billy's incompetence that Ida had begun to develop to explain her own interview. The guy did in fact know all the bland questions to ask. This realization left her confused and self-conscious. Had she said something wrong?

She sat silently as Sally made her case before the tribunal of one that would determine her mettle under fire and her general suitableness for a minimum wage job. And Sally made her case well, with airy responses, demure looks, and some technical knowledge.

Ida found herself wishing Sally would screw up and be condemned to a life of perpetual unemployment. She began to study the faded and torn posters on the walls: cartoons about the need for safe behaviour. Insulting, she decided, for implying that cartoons were needed for factory floor employees to understand that they shouldn't mutilate themselves. Companies, she noted, don't put that kind of crap on the walls of their offices. In the office area of The Plastic Man there were posters of inspirational slogans set against backgrounds of waterfalls, sunsets, and kittens hanging from tree branches. Not a single poster warned people not to stick their fingers into pencil sharpeners.

She began to study her resume that had been tossed onto the table. It was upside down but she could read Bill's notes. There were only two. The first said, *'bit of a gut'*, and the second read, *'trace of b o'*.

She stared at the page for a long time, her face reddening. She started to get to her feet but quickly sat back down. She looked at her waist, turned her head to the side and surreptitiously breathed deep, but smelled nothing untoward.

Neither Sally nor the foreman appeared to notice.

Ida drove her twenty-year-old unlicensed car through traffic. She'd only taken it today rather than face a one-hour bus ride in the early morning. She accelerated, waited at a light, gunned it, stopped, waited, waited, waited, until she was ready to scream. She would pass eight-hundred and fifty-seven signs on the way home directing her about what she could or couldn't do. Around her, drivers ran red lights and took corners by cutting through parking lots, frustrated, turning into road-raging petty criminals. Even when control exists with the best of intentions it is human nature to resist it.

Today Ida felt the frustration of driving as just more humiliation. Just more banal totalitarian power that strips one of self-governance, like the Taylorism at The Plastic Man, like bully bosses, and even like the billboards she passed of people on Caribbean beaches telling her what to dream.

She resented the failure of her dreams and the carrot the ads dangled that kept her toiling at crap jobs. She felt an overwhelming anger at the million humiliations that came from simply living her drab, powerless existence.

4.

I'd lift my skirts for this guy

Louis drove through the countryside where he'd grown up. Like a migratory bird he always returned. This was not a destination but the absence of one. This was the elephant's graveyard where people in his family came to die. Home was a cemetery plot in all respects.

Passing some road workers prompted him to tell Joseph about the time his older brother Larry, and Larry's friend, had stolen a huge grader when they were teenagers. They had driven for two blocks, past the high school, with Larry's buddy sitting in the space where the passenger seat would have been, as casual as if this was a beer run and he'd called 'shotgun'. Not to be outdone for pure savoir-faire, Larry drove with his left arm draped over the frame of an open window, his sleeve rolled up. It was the same naked arm that had once been used to demonstrate, for Louis, how skin could be covered in butane, then lit, without causing any damage.

The story tailed off.

Beside him, Joseph didn't appear to be listening. He was staring at the bush, mesmerized.

"You fantasizing?" Louis asked.

"Yeah, that I'm on a horse runnin' beside the car. Sometimes you gotta jump ditches and avoid stuff. You ever notice how, if you look right, sideways at the trees, that they smear together, like a blur?"

"Yeah, but the best thing is to look down. It gives the sensation you're moving a million miles an hour."

Joseph rolled down his window and hung his head out to look down at the gravel shoulder.

Louis turned up the radio to drown out the windstorm now whipping about inside the car. Chet Atkins was singing.

"Man, if I was a chick I'd lift my skirts for this guy," Louis said emphatically.

"The wind's givin' me an earache," replied Joseph and he rolled up the window.

Louis turned down the radio. "So that's all you've been

thinkin' about for the past hour; that you're on a horse and jumpin' shit on the shoulder?"

"Naw. I'm thinking there may be a party at Kyle's tonight cus it's Saturday. We gonna be home by tonight?"

"Long before that."

"Good. I was remembering Kyle's parties. They're always way out of control." Joseph giggled at the thought. "People talk about em for weeks on end afterwards. The bacon always shows up, so you gotta have a stomach for that and for some fightin' with the neighbours." He began to bounce the back of his head against the seat while he talked.

The car stopped at a red light in the centre of a six street town.

Louis glanced at Joseph. "What's with you? You look like a jumping flea with a yeast infection."

Joseph said nothing.

When the light turned to green and the car ahead didn't move, Louis hit the horn and yelled, "Let's go Sparky!" Then, in his usual volume, added, "His parents must give him major shit. They still let him have parties?"

"Naw, but he does anyway. They yap at him when they get home and Kyle always promises to be a good boy. He puts on his hangdog face and they forgive him. But as soon as they go away again it's the same thing all over. I feel sorry for him. Last party I went to, I went back to his place on Sunday morning, you know, to help with the clean up. It was a fuck of a mess: beer bottles and crap everywhere. There was me, Lily, Kevin, Rick and Bennie. It was one of the best clean-ups ever." Joseph began to laugh at what was to come, and it soon took an effort to talk. "There were… (giggle, snort) there were… (giggle) there were clothes people had left, all kinds of broken crap, and in the middle of a huge pile of empties was a dead goat. I swear." Boisterous laughter spilled over the restraints and he rocked his head with even more flea-like aggression.

Louis laughed along.

After Joseph calmed, he added with judicial caution, "If there's a party and a clean-up it'd be good to get Ren. Maybe he can be convinced to come. That'd be great if we got him.

We don't want Leo. One time Kevin brought him because Leo was the goalie on his hockey team. He's supposed to be a great fuckin' goalie but I don't know what that's gotta do with cleanin'. Like there's supposed to be skills you learn on the rink that'll help you clean. Maybe if you drive the Zamboni, I guess. But his cleanin' technique was to bring over bottles: a whole case of old cologne and aftershave. His father owns that perfume outlet store in the mall on Highway 21, so Leo got the stale shit and brought it. Instead of washing stuff, he sprayed perfume into every nook and cranny to kill the smell of tobacco, weed and puke. The rest of us had to open every door and bring out some fans to try and get the air breathable again. Even after that the place still stank like a salesman's convention. At least he left his fuckin' skates at home."

Louis shook his head and smiled, but he felt a sudden sadness. He knew Joseph wasn't going to be going to any parties any time soon. Just the thought of being 'home' was making him antsy.

"I'm gonna go in here and make a call," Louis said, pulling into a gas station.

Instead of driving up to the pumps, he parked the Capri alongside the variety store.

Joseph tensed and he watched Louis's hands. Happily, there was nothing in them. No gun.

Louis climbed out of the Capri but didn't go inside. He went to the phone booth at the corner of the building, dug around in his pocket, put a quarter in the phone and dialled a number. With casual bravado he draped an arm over the phone while it rang, turned, and watched the highway traffic. There was an intermittent whoosh of vehicles speeding by but he heard Ida clearly say, "Yes?" She'd picked up the receiver part way through the first ring having just set it down.

"Guess who?" said Louis.

Hesitation. "You! I can't believe it." Her tone was suddenly convivial and bright. Force of habit with respect to Louis, no doubt. But then, with memories kicking in, her voice quickly resumed its edge. "What the fuck happened? Last time you were here, six months ago, it was like (and her tone dropped an octave in imitation of Louis) 'Yeah babe, I'm

24

gonna call you in a few weeks'."

"Yeah, well sorry."

Ida knew from experience that the bastard had a childish aw shucks smirk on his stupid face.

"It's not a problem. I like being humiliated," she said. "For three years it's been you promising me things and never delivering."

"Eh?" This was not like Ida; she was ego-soothing and never voiced any serious dissatisfaction with him. (Aside to the reader: This fact, according to her friend Sally, was based on Ida's fear of rejection, the belief that she would be dumped if she proved to be anything less than perfect. Never complain. Never look less than your best. Sally also found Ida's inability to acknowledge the selfishness of Louis's behaviour truly confounding, and wondered if Ida avoided judging it in the knowledge that it might lead to self-contempt for tolerating his actions.)

"Never mind. I just heard I didn't get a job I applied for. I'm pissed off. The asshole that did the interview had his back to me the whole time and only asked three or four lame ass questions."

"He had his back to you? That's a new one."

"He was just going through the fucking motions. I knew I wasn't going to get it. He was only interested in Sally. The whole fucking job search thing is humiliating. You let someone judge you. They have all the power and you're kissing their ass."

"So why you lookin' for a new job?"

That Louis would need to ask this question annoyed Ida. He knew nothing about her while she had spent thousands of hours over the last three years thinking about him. But she dismissed the thought in a moment. "The plastics place laid off a bunch of us. I guess if business picks back up we'll get called in."

"Really! Shit! That sucks... So I guess you're not doing nothin' right now?"

"No, not at the moment. Oh, you mean in general. No, not doing anything 'cept looking for a job. What about you?"

"Same old."

"Just doing your thing, eh? Where are you?"

"'Bout ten kilometres away. Just bringing Joseph back."

"So let me get this right. You had time to come by and get Joseph but not to call me?" The hardness in her voice that had begun to soften, returned.

"I did call but you didn't answer and you don't have no answering machine. Anyway, I'm calling cus I was gonna ask if you wanted some company. But now I'm thinking that, seeing as you're not working, maybe you wanna come with me."

"For how long?"

"A few weeks. Take a break from the stress."

"I don't know if I can. I need to make some money."

"Don't you have EI?"

"It's not like I can live on that."

"Okay, two weeks then. I have a few bucks. I can cover things."

Hesitation.

"You got a boyfriend?" Louis asked, trying to sort it out.

"Kinda. It's not serious… Where you planning on going?"

"Just drive round, take in some of the scenery, maybe do some fishin'."

"In your ratty old van?"

"No, no. I got a car now and I have family we can stay with."

Ida didn't respond immediately. "So when did you say you were gonna be here?"

"I don't know; twenty minutes."

There was another hesitation. "Yeah, okay. That'll be nice," she finally replied sweetly.

"What's one more fucking humiliation?" she said aloud after hanging up the phone, pissed off once again. "One more asshole thinks he can call you up when he's around and then ignore you afterwards."

She would have to make something up to explain her absence to Keith; slide a note under his door.

The guilt that set in was immediately soothed by the recollection that just that morning she'd been considering ending it with him, perhaps prompted by the possibility of getting a job and regaining a degree of normalcy in her life. There was something about him that made her uneasy. He had said he was self-employed but the last time she was at his place she'd picked up some opened mail off the coffee table when he went to the washroom. Sandwiched between a pizza flyer and a VISA bill was a cheque from social assistance. It could be for any number of things, including mental disability, not that it mattered, everyone has problems at times. It was the fact he'd lied that made her uneasy.

She had to rush. She got a piece of paper and scribbled a note.

5.

her almond skin was devoid of subtext

At eleven AM Keith got out of bed and on his way to the can noticed a piece of paper that had been slid under the front door.

'Gone to visit my mother. Back in a few weeks.'

"Shit," he muttered, and vigorously rubbed the top of his head with his right hand, as if needing more circulation for his brain to function. He read the note again before detouring to the window and looking down toward the front entrance. There was nothing going on beyond the usual comings and goings. "Shit," he said again.

After staring at the sidewalk for a time, apparently locked in a mental vacuum, he went to the bathroom and then to the bedroom where he got dressed.

He exited the apartment and took the elevator downstairs.

Five or six residents were once again standing around the lobby, but conversing in normal volumes, unlike the night before. One or two people looked familiar but Keith focused so little on those around him that he was never sure whether he'd seen someone before or not. A couple of residents nodded in his direction as he made his way to the mailboxes, tragedy seemingly causing the first stirrings of some sort of community feeling among the tenants. He paused with his mailbox door open, listening to the conversations.

A fast-talking teenager, with hair the colour of a ripe cantaloupe, was telling the group that the name of the dead man was Stonewall Jackson Cutter, but the guy went by the name of Stone. Stone Cutter, the guy said, had once told him that his mother had given her Civil War re-enactor brother carte blanche in naming her new baby.

"I never met him," announced the teenager's female companion in a strident voice, looking about with a beaming, moon face. She wore a small, tight-fitting dress and her almond skin was devoid of subtext.

No one replied, their attention diverted by a seventyish-looking woman who'd gotten off the elevator and was now

28

making a beeline for the group. She clearly had something to say. "I was just talking to Bessie, the old lady who lives next door to the boy who died," the woman began, and to no one in particular added, "you know the one."

"Stone," said the kid.

"What a name, eh?" laughed his friend, again looking around for approval.

"Huh?" The old woman was bewildered. "Oh, no, not the boy. I mean the old lady I was talking to: Bessie. She's in a wheelchair? Always well turned out?" She looked around for some sign that the group knew who Bessie was. Nothing. "Anyway, Bessie was talking to the Super and he told her the police think the young lad who died was murdered, so they're going to keep the apartment shut up for a few days." She nodded vigorously as if to say, 'yes it's true'.

There were horrified looks.

"I believe it. I was watchin' the cops comin' in and was pretty sure there was a whole hive of forensics people." The speaker was a small Methuselah in a dirty yellow sweater.

"I knew that's what it was," said a man with a cane, as if vindicated. "It's the Hayes gang. My son says he seen Stone hanging out with them a coupla times. They got a farm on County Road 18, a mile or so south, that place on the right with the big red barn." He pointed over his shoulder toward the huge windows behind him. "My son says they make drugs there."

"How's your son know?" asked the teen with the cantaloupe hair, smirking at the cleverness of his insinuation.

"I've never met a gang member," added his lady friend in a booming voice, continuing her insistence on narrating her non-involvement.

"Everybody hears the stories goin' round when they're young and have a social life – like my son," tersely answered the guy with the cane. "Hate to see a young guy like that get killed, his whole life in front of him, but he was a punk and ya live like a punk ya gotta accept what happens."

6.

fuckin' Catholics

Louis and Ida drove north, through cottage country. It was late afternoon when they got to Keats Bay. They detoured through it to find a restaurant.

"My friend, Peter Dubey, was telling me the other day that he discovered this area many years ago – late 1960s – when he got busted as he stepped off the train after coming up here from down south," said Louis.

"Like Columbus discovering America, eh?" Ida meant this to be gentle teasing.

"Yeah. Same thing. Peter discovered the place. He was a real imperialist and pioneer."

"I meant that as a joke. So you think he discovered it? People have been living here for a long time."

"But his getting arrested here, with weed in his suitcase, was the beginning of the place as a modern city. Like all imperialists, he brought modern civilization – to everyone's detriment."

Ida took in the store windows of Main Street, and wondered. She had heard Louis talk about Peter once before, on the day of his funeral years ago. And yet here Louis was, saying the two had recently been conversing. Like he spoke to spirits. His weirdness always blew over if you weathered it.

"How's your Joseph doing?" She smiled, brightening at the thought of him, as she reached over and squeezed Louis's right hand, which was laying on the car seat. She began to walk her fingers up his arm but he pulled it away and put his hand back on the wheel.

"Good," Louis said distractedly, and then with conviction, "Good."

Ida turned her head to the right to look in the direction of a couple on the sidewalk. "I guess he's out of the hospital now," she said, trying to conceal her feelings, but a degree of hurt was still present in her tone.

"Nope. He just took a holiday."

30

Ida watched a group of woman on the sidewalk and wondered whether they faced the same fucking humiliations as her: guys that took you for granted, getting ordered around at work, interviewing for a job with an asshole who doesn't hire you because he's only looking for hot women, even obedient shopping (like these women might be doing) for things they've been told they must have. Suckers all, who will have buyer's remorse about all the crap they bought. And not just about the merchandise but for all the nonsense they bought into about what is normal and desirable.

She allowed herself a momentary fantasy about the day Louis would grovel in front of her after she responded to one of his phone calls by telling him to piss off.

About a minute or so later, Ida picked up the thread of the conversation in a lighter, conciliatory tone. "So you busted our boy out."

"That's about it, 'cept we didn't bust anything. It takes no great genius to get someone outta there."

"Guess he needed a break."

"More like I missed him. He's got such a rich imagination he doesn't need to go anywhere."

"What did they say when you took him back? Guess they were furious, eh?"

"I didn't take him back; just dropped him a block away like always. What he does is his business, after I drop him off, but he always just goes back to the hospital. You could see the nerves takin' over the closer we got."

"Poor kid. You think he'll ever get discharged?"

"Doubt it. His family's moved away."

As they drove on in silence, Louis recalled an incident from two years before when Joseph was driving the car. He had come up on a sinkhole in the road, a big gaping thing, and only stopped at the last minute when Louis and the guys in the back seat had yelled at him. Joseph was obviously embarrassed but he, Louis, had made things worse by ordering the kid to pull over and then swapping spots with him. "Better let me take over the driving before you kill someone," he'd said to some laughs from the back seat denizens. He wished now he hadn't done that. Fuck he hated himself sometimes. Every fucking memory tormented him with no distinction between the significant and the meaningless. This moral conscience that we're supposed to have, or so we are told, had begun to run wild on Louis and to turn on him for everything he'd ever done in life, for trying to be popular, for doing what it took to get by, for just living. Worst of all was that every memory provoked feelings of humiliation and regret, and in the vast majority of cases it was over harmless behaviour; the sort of things that people say or do without thinking.

"What about you? You think you'll ever end up back in a psych ward?" Ida broke the quiet.

"Nope, never. I never was clinically depressed anyway. You?"

"Of course. I'm going this summer like I always do, just to get my medication right."

"I always thought it was a hell of way to spend your vacation."

"Not for me. Free food and drugs. Sympathy. Sometimes I just get so fucking pissed off I need to cool down."

Louis shook his head. "I don't believe in taking any sort of psychiatric drugs. I understand why people take them though. Fear and unhappiness are pretty compelling motives. Every odd feeling of unknown origin brings with it a fear of death. Me, I want to deal with that when it happens. Medications just numb me to the presence of death in life. Drugs work for others sometimes, I know, but what really bothers me is that the medical profession's first response to anything is often to look for the right pill to fix you. Lazy fucks."

"Ah…" Ida began and then passed over whatever it was she was about to say. "You know, going to the psych hospital is not really my idea of the ideal vacation," she added. "Sally and I keep dreaming of going to Cuba. There was a poster of a beach resort in the coffee shop across the road from The Plastic Man and the daydream of us laying on the white sand helped us deal with all the bullshit."

Louis said nothing. This sort of thing mystified him. Not because he didn't appreciate dreams but because he did. Most people used dreams to escape the 'shittiness of life', as Louis often put it, but he wanted to integrate dreams into his life. He even began his day with them. It was why he was friends with Joseph. The kid would weep or become depressed with his fantasies. Dreams were the present and not the future. Dreams were real. Louis understood the poetry of life when wrapped in dreams. Sure, he had his own escapism, but that was by running away, not by creating an alternative present to avoid the bad parts of life.

"You ever worry those fuckers won't let you out?" Louis asked.

"For depression? No. Not for someone who's checked themselves in." Ida said this with the lawyerly conviction of experience.

"I always think 'bout that woman in the secure section with Joseph when I was first there," Louis said, "before he was moved to the regular area with you and me. They went to court to take away her freedom and force her to stay in the hospital. She was supposed to be sick in the head cuz she'd tell em to go to hell."

"Gertrude. Yeah, well, she was pretty paranoid. Remember she'd throw her tray of food on the floor and say they were trying to poison her. You gotta get with the game, play along, no matter what your truth is; don't say what you really think. You can't be different. Different, to them, means you're sick. But yeah, you're right, you shouldn't be locked up like an animal or a murderer just for being different."

"I've seen lots of people on the outside like her. If that's mental illness they should lock up those fuckers who think Muslims are all terrorists out to get us. Bigotry actually can do a lot of harm, unlike Gertrude."

"Don't tell me you let yourself argue with wackos like that?"

"Naw. Even well-meaning criticism can have a reverse effect and help the person sneak by. Like the wackjob cult leader. When he's told why people reject him he hides the extreme sections of his platform when speaking in public and just expresses what's sorta normal. Listen to politicians and you'll see what I mean."

"I don't…"

"So you miss your job?" Louis seemed anxious to change the subject.

"No way. It's sweltering in there and you can't even get a drink of water. Now they put in a new system to force you to work faster. You have to scan everything with an RF gun. The supervisor looks at the stats all through the day and if they don't think you've done enough in the last hour they come and talk to you, like, 'Why did you only do half your quota?'. One foreman asked me that and I told him 'Cus I have diarrhoea.' He blushed and walked away. Serves him right. They're idiots. They want you to be a team, but they punish you if you do anything to help your co-worker cus that reduces your productivity. They're teaching that it's every man for himself in spite of what they say."

"They wanna keep you scared for your job," said Louis. "That's the new normal. People can't turn their brains off and work flat out for eight hours the way that those moronic engineers think they can. It's dehumanizing and leads to mistakes, but people try to do it cus they're afraid of gettin' fired."

Ida stared out the window, not registering the houses nor responding. "There's no fucking privacy anymore," she continued eventually. "They want to police you every minute of the day. And monitor you. The company's next step, I heard, is gonna be to put a bunch of cameras in to spy on people." She frowned and her attention returned to what they were passing. "Some nice places here." But the distraction was brief. "And there's no way out of getting treated like dirt. Not only am I now looking for another crap job but it's looking like I'll have to beg for one. Maybe sleep with the boss…cus I've got to find something to pay the rent!" She bitterly rolled down her window a couple of centimetres. "Even so, I'm glad in a way I didn't get the job I interviewed for this morning. The supervisor is a real asshole. Bill Lisle's his name. Treats you like a piece of shit. He asks me a few questions and then starts sucking up to Sally. I saw his notes and the only thing he wrote down was about how I looked and even how I smelled! He was interviewing women and judging their suitability based solely on their looks."

"That's fucked up. There's got to be a better way to make money than working in shit jobs... Did Sally get hired?"

"I don't know. I didn't talk to her. But yeah, of course she did, old Billy Boy is looking to get laid."

"Guess he couldn't tell she's a dyke."

"No," Ida laughed loudly at this small measure of vengeance. "She'll play him though. She knows how to do that."

They stopped at a crosswalk leading to a square in front of an expansive Catholic church. A thin fortyish-looking man passed in front of them.

"Son of a bitch," said Louis, craning his head forward. "That's Bestial Bernie." He began to roll his window down but something stopped him.

"Bestial Bernie?" Ida said.

"Yeah, a guy I used to go to high school with. Poor bastard always got beat up cus everyone knew how he liked to screw the animals on his farm."

"Jesus!"

"Yeah. Fuckin' Catholics. Chastity is unnatural."

They drove on in silence.

Like the hunger pang that suddenly invades and overwhelms you with misery, Louis remembered a sunny day some twenty-five years before when he was walking down the main street of this same city. He'd walked out in front of a car driven by an old man, and looked directly into the guy's terrified eyes a moment before the man swung the car violently to the right to avoid hitting him, and drove straight into the front window of a store. Louis had continued across the road and walked on to his destination as if nothing had happened. He was too stoned on his first meds to register what was happening.

Louis quickly turned these thoughts away and began to play with the radio.

7.

a bullet between Al's confused eyes

Restaurant owner Jack Hayes sawed through an immense hunk of bleeding meat then took a swig from a glass of pricey merlot. His stool was parked next to a high butcher-block counter in the back of his steakhouse. The counter was cleared of pots and pans from the dinner service, and now served as a table for Jack and his guest, Al Jackson, sitting on his right, pushing gnocchi around his plate while laboriously chewing. Al was only slightly overweight but wheezed from the effort of eating. Between them was the merlot bottle, a plate of sliced tomatoes, a cheese board with a huge hunk of parmesan on it, a grater, and an oversized knife, apparently for slicing the rock hard cheese if anyone's greed got the better of them.

Jack smacked his lips in a way meant to induce envy, rolled his eyes and said, "Fuck this is good man. I tell you Al, you gotta try a steak. They're from my own cows. We slaughter them on the farm ourselves. Only the best Angus cattle and we don't pump them full of antibiotics neither."

Al eyed Jack's bleeding steak with the sad expression of an unwilling celibate. It was beckoning to him with its siren call. "My eyes say 'yes' but my heart doc says 'no'."

"Too bad." Jack eyed Al's paunch and his gaze travelled north to take in the large blue and red nose with its Metro map of spider veins. What he saw was a swelled head and a broken body. Pathetic, he thought, these physical wrecks who want to wield power over others, probably to compensate for their own physical impotence.

"At least throw a slice of tomato on your plate," Jack said. "They're from the farm too. We dump the cow shit on the garden; that's why they're so big."

The dinner meeting was informal but Jack – who liked to schmooze with the more well-heeled types in his restaurant – wore a $3000 suit, as he invariably did.

The absent cook staff had been told to stay out of the kitchen until further notice and to loiter at the back of the

36

dining room where they should try not to stare at the last table of customers lingering over desert and drinks. The guests would be advised that the kitchen was closed should they order anything else.

Jack casually picked up the menacing cheese knife – which wouldn't be out of place doing duty as a scythe at the farm – and sliced himself a sliver of parmesan, then installed it in his mouth.

"Listen Jocko," said Al abruptly, in an aggressive tone that belied the apparent affability that had existed until then. "I'm not gonna keep telling you. Stop it with the E production. We've been over this twice already and I'm not gonna tell you again." His aggressiveness seemed to ebb. "But like I been saying, you wanna work for us, now that's another story. I like having a mutually beneficial relationship with others – like your cozy arrangement with the Triceps."

"And that's what I wanted to discuss. I'm a businessman, as long as I can make a good profit off it the details of something aren't important. We've bin out of the manufacturing business for awhile but we have a nice network of buyers."

Behind Jack was the deep fryer and he could feel its prickly heat. He wiped the faint trace of sweat off his face with an open hand to mask his expression of loathing in case it was showing. He was giving the customers what they wanted; running a fair business. Free enterprise. Who was this fat prick to tell him what he could or couldn't do?

"Fuck that cheese is good," Jack added theatrically and made a melodramatic display of attempting to cut another slice while apparently meeting some resistance.

"That's a start but I don't buy…"

"Jesuz fuckin' Christ!" Jack yelped, dropping the knife on the counter as he stood up, knocking his stool sideways. Blood ran from the palm of his left hand that he was holding out in front of him. Broad splotches fell on the counter, on his steak, and over his $500 shoes.

"Help me!" he begged Al who had risen to his feet, his mouth fallen stupidly open.

"What do I do?" Al squeaked.

"Give me your napkin and get that knife the fuck away from me." Jack waved at the incriminating utensil as if it was about to attack him.

Al snatched up his large crisply starched cloth napkin and handed it to Jack then gingerly picked up the knife as if it had satanic qualities.

Jack wrapped the napkin around his wounded hand then deliberately stepped backward against the deep fryer and shoved his right elbow into it. He uttered a deep, shocked gasp and screamed.

Al stood immobilized with his hand still extended, holding the knife, and something like terror in his wide bewildered eyes.

The kitchen staff and the diners froze, all eyes shifting toward the kitchen door. Chef Patrick, who had been on edge, annoyed at being shut out of his own kitchen, jumped to his feet, as did Carlo, the only waiter still new enough to give a damn.

Before anyone could get to the kitchen door, Jack reached to the shelf above the deep fryer and with his undamaged hand grabbed a pistol hidden behind a huge can of fat drippings. He pulled out the handgun and put a bullet between Al's confused eyes.

Al went down with the knife still in his hand.

Jack immediately let the gun fall to the floor.

As staff and customers in the dining room began to sprint for the exit, a visibly frightened Chef Patrick peeked through the small window in the kitchen door. He looked into the eyes of Jack who was waving him forward. The chef pushed open the door and was followed into the kitchen by sous chef Carlo.

Jack staggered towards them, tears in his eyes. "Get an ambulance," he pled, "get me some fucking napkins, and for the love of God fill me a bucket full of ice water." As he dropped to his knees he could hear Al's man outside in the back alley kicking the locked, metal back door. "And get a rag to clean my shoes," he muttered faintly.

When he was finally interviewed by two detectives, three

hours later in hospital, Jack Hayes was still suffering from the fryer burn but the fact that he could push away the pain enough to coherently converse (albeit laboriously) was testament to the quality of the morphine. His only concern at that moment was staying awake long enough to deliver his lines.

Fortunately for him, what he was about to relate was something he'd been rehearsing for two days; since Al Jackson requested a meeting. Jack's staging of his little drama had gone stupendously; the delivery perfect. The mangled elbow was unfortunate but it argued credibility like nothing else could. Al had said he wanted to negotiate a business deal but Jack knew that this meant that Al would always be the one calling the shots. He'd showed Al who not to fuck with. Gave him a taste of his own.

It was now on to the final act.

The story, as Jack told it, was that Al had picked up a large knife off the table and come after him but he had grabbed hold of the blade in self-defence. (That Al's corpse was still clutching the bloody knife and that there was a deep gash across the palm of Jack's left hand would eventually confirm this as a fact in the minds of the detectives.) Jack told how he had struggled and in the process was pushed backward against the deep fryer, his elbow eventually being shoved into it. He had screamed. He couldn't help it. It felt like he'd stumbled into hell.

"I suddenly remembered," Jack said in an increasingly slurred monotone, "that we keep a pistol on the shelf above the fryer. It's been there for six months since had a robbery one night when someone came in with a gun and stole a case of wine. Can't believe I thought of it with all the shit going down but I did. Anyways, I grabbed the thing and shot the bastard. Hitting him was blind luck. I couldn't see for the tears in my eyes. I got him though."

"What set Mr. Jackson off? Why did he attack you?" asked Detective Swain.

"Nothing. Leasts I don't know what it was."

"You always have meetings in the kitchen?"

"Sometimes. The staff can tell you better than me how

often. We were talkin' about somethin' private so I didn't want to meet in the restaurant where someone might hear."

"What were you talking about?"

"Like I said, it was private. Guess Al didn't like what he heard."

Swain exchanged glances with his partner. It was perhaps a question about whether now was the time to push Hayes – who they both knew to be a lying bastard – or not; the guy was in pain and his speech was plodding.

"Okay, we're going to take off but we'll be back tomorrow. Whether there's charges against you or not will depend on what we find in the kitchen."

Jack watched them leave and, despite the pain, smirked as the door closed behind them. Charges, he thought, just what the fuck are they going to charge me with?

"Do you believe that shit about suddenly remembering he had a gun on the shelf?" Swain asked his partner as they walked down the hospital corridor.

"Well, the kitchen staff all said that there was a gun on the shelf since the robbery, so it's possible. And the robbery is why the back door is now kept locked. Hayes could be telling the truth for once in his life. I mean, who's likely to shove their own arm into a deep fryer and scar themselves for life? It just doesn't happen, especially not with a guy like that: he's a real fucking dandy. And besides, they're all cowards, really, punks like that."

8.

she's small but shifty fast

Louis switched off the ignition and in a pleased tone pronounced, "We're here."

Ida, who'd been fitfully dozing, with her seat in recline, gripped the bottom of the door window and raised her head in a Kilroy-was-here moment.

They were parked in front of a small house, somewhere in the country. The building appeared to be made up of three sections. While the additions were mere silhouettes, two patches of light illuminated the main house. A bare bulb above the exterior door cast a circle of amber light on a tiny porch, and a yellow-drenched scene was visible through the living room window, a tableau framed by the house and the opaque surrounding forest.

Looking back through the car's rear window, Ida saw the scattered lights of a nearby town atop a hill in the distance.

A car hissed past on the highway and both she and Louis glanced at it. In the country, every vehicle is an event.

"So this is Grandma's eh?" said Ida.

"It is."

As they climbed from the car, Ida was revived by the coolness of a breeze brushing her face. Looking through the front window of the house, she saw a tiny older woman (her permed grey head barely visible above the sill) walking back and forth, conversing either to herself or to someone unseen.

The slam of the Capri's doors caused the old woman to stop, startled. She went to the window, moving her face close, squinting into the impenetrable darkness.

Ida smiled back, unsure if the old lady could see her.

Louis, who had walked to Ida's side of the car, took her hand and led her towards the house. They climbed the three stairs of the porch.

The expression of the woman at the window was intense, her head jabbing back and forth like a bird's, trying to make out what was going on outside.

Louis rapped three times at the door causing the old lady

to look to her right and to finally spot him, now only a metre away.

Grandma's reaction was visceral repulsion followed by fury. She vigorously shook her head, mouthed the word 'no' and began a backhanded wave to shoo him away. The picture window was framed by a tall narrow window on each side that could be opened a few inches. After aggressively twisting the swivel handle of one of them, Grandma turned her head sideways, put her mouth to the narrow opening and yelled through the screen. "You! You get out! Get out! Get away from here!"

"Aw c'mon Grandma, it's Louie! We've come a long way just to see you."

"Get out of here!" the old lady bellowed. "You're no grandson of mine!" She stepped back, twisted the window shut, and spoke to herself with enough volume to still be audible to the pair outside. "That's it, I'm calling the police." With that, she pirouetted and disappeared from view.

Ida pulled on Louis's hand as she stepped back out of the circle of light, but he resisted, his face now divided by light and dark. He was grinning.

"C'mon," said Ida. "Let's go. Grandma's calling the cops for real."

Louis remained still, despite the tugs, until finally yelling, "Okay Grandma! We're leaving. Love you!"

The pair retreated to the Capri.

Louis continued to smirk as he backed the car down the driveway having enjoyed the encounter with Grandma very much.

"What the hell did you do to her, you bastard?" asked Ida with indulgence rather than recrimination, picking up on Louie's mood.

He laughed. "I may have borrowed some money."

"May have?! Stole if from her I think you mean."

"I'm going to pay it back."

"She's a feisty old broad," said Ida.

"Yeah, she was always like that: strict. When we were kids she'd would chase after us if we didn't do what we were told and then wallop us with her broom. She's small but shifty fast and could really pack a wallop. 'Raging Raylene' we used to call her."

As they drove on, Ida pondered the old lady's reaction to her grandson with growing sympathy. Old people didn't have a lot of money and Louie could be a bit of a parasite; not surprising given his upbringing. He'd had to resort to any means at hand to get by. Whatever love you feel gets shunted aside and everyone becomes a mark. And if you don't feel loved you figure the only way you'll get anything out of anyone is to scam them. Grandmothers always forgive their grandkids no matter what, so Louis must have really taken her for a ride.

Ida wasn't privy to any information concerning Louis's finances. She understood that he had closed his business two years before but he talked like he still lived in the same house, outside the city. How could he do that with no income? But she didn't pursue the thought, as always.

"Granny looks pretty good. How old is she?"

"No idea," Louis brushed the question aside. "Let me put on some music." And he became engaged with twisting knobs.

Ida briefly considered the question herself. The old lady should be around ninety, based on Louis's age, but she looked more like seventy. If she was, it would mean that she was in her mid to late twenties when she became a grandmother. Impossible in all but theory. Ida didn't pursue the question. It wasn't her business after all, she told herself.

9.

someone you'd expect to see masturbating in a park

The cops declined to set up anywhere in the proximity of Jack Hayes's farm before the raid went down. There was no quiet positioning nearby that might tip off the occupants about what was to happen. Instead, the swat team assembled a kilometre away before commencing their blitzkrieg.

The convoy paused briefly at the front gate, at the foot of a long dirt drive, while someone jumped out of the lead car to open the gate and drag it across the ground.

It was three-hundred metres from there, up an incline, to a stucco farmhouse sitting perpendicular to the driveway.

At the house, the lead car gravel-slid to a stop. Three other vehicles swung right, immediately before the house, turning onto a dirt path that was usually only travelled by hay wagons and tractors. They skipped over a mild rise, through a slight dip, and came to a hard stop in front of a blood red barn.

On their left, a chained German Shepherd barked insanely. It rocketed forward to be suddenly stopped in mid leap, suspended in the air by its restraint before yo-yoing back to where it had begun. Over and over it lunged with crazed bloodlust.

A huge collie bounded out from behind the house and planted its front paws on the chest of the first officer to get out of his car. Upright, the dog came to the man's chin. The officer struggled to unholster his gun. The dog, tail wagging furiously, then pounced on a second cop and sent him staggering, but the guy knew what was happening, that this was a greeting. "Settle down there killer," he laughed.

Unknown to the police was the fact that a camera, in an oak tree near the highway, had picked up their party the moment they stopped at the front gate. The biker watching the security monitors had immediately flicked on a blue light bulb in the basement lab below the barn. A bell briefly rang and the four bikers, working around a long stainless steel table, lifted their heads momentarily. A couple of the men guffawed and one swore, "Suck it pigs." They all laughed and went back to work.

The two bikers, upstairs in the barn, went through a frequently rehearsed exercise to block off a huge circular concrete pipe whose opening was in the floor, in the middle of the barn. It led down to the drug lab below.

Eighteen seconds after the first police car appeared and the alarm sounded, one of the bikers, laying on his stomach, dropped a metal plate into the pipe, positioning it on a ledge that ran around the inside periphery, half way down. Beneath the ledge, the metal ladder, attached to the concrete wall, that led to the bunker below, was no longer visible.

With the false bottom in place, the biker positioned a waterproof liner over it.

Hoisting himself back up into the barn, he dumped five buckets of filthy water into the hole. These were kept at hand for just such an occasion.

He then dragged a metal plate over the concrete hole to give it the appearance – if it was discovered – that it was a drain. The second man shovelled dirt into the cracks around the edges of the plate, to hide its presence, and threw some hay and manure over it.

Next, his partner removed a piece of fencing at the end of the cow's pen. With the fencing down, the area for the cattle (the quarter of the herd that was always kept inside for just this eventuality) was greatly expanded.

One of the men grabbed a switch and shooed the steakhouse cattle along. With much mooing and jostling, they ambled forward into the space and all trace of the entrance to the bunker below was now gone.

What the police found when they swept into the barn, seconds later, was a couple of rustic looking farmers. One, it was noted by a cop, looked like the guy in Whistler's famous painting. He should have, his outfit was sold in dozens of costume supply shops. Dressing his barn manager in it (and pointing to the fraudulence of the farmers) was Jack Hayes's idea of a joke on the police.

Down below, the bikers in the lab were now quiet. One of them, Lemony, had switched off the expensive ventilation system. Without it, all production had stopped and the men, following emergency protocol, were now shuffling down a tunnel to its other end, well beyond the barn, where there was a vent directly to the outside. No one would have wanted to stay in any case, because without the fans it was not only dangerous but the smell from Kenny would be intolerable. He always removed his obligatory black t-shirt and hung it behind him when he worked. The odour of sweat from his flab then wafted about the room like a medieval miasma.

"That's them tryin' to catch us by surprise, thinkin' we'll be unprepared without Jack here," Kenny said softly, being a master of the obvious. With his sketchy appearance he looked like someone you'd expect to see masturbating in a park.

"Yep," agreed Fish, so called because he looked normal from the side, but when viewed from the front he was freakishly narrow, like a smallish ten-year-old body placed on the legs of a six-footer.

The guys here were low level biker gang members, mostly young, mostly dull, with the exception of the handsome one with long blonde locks who they called Lemony. He struggled with his conscience for making street drugs, would one day live in China, translate the poetry of Li Bai, and frequently rail against what he considered to be Ezra Pound's 'anglocentrism' in that one's translations.

"You'd think, after the last time when they couldn't find a lab, that they'd a given up," said Kenny. Sweat was beading up and glistening on his shaved head. "They don't even know anyone's here cus they're suckered by the shell game."

No one commented. Fish smirked to himself because of Kenny's denseness, which was observed by Lemony, who also smiled, and shared a conspiratorial grin with Wayne. Kenny was oblivious.

The three vehicles owned by the farm were driven in and out daily to mask from the watching cops that there was anything different happening at the farm during the days when the Ecstasy lab was up and running. Every day was made to look the same. The cops could only conclude that supplies and product were moving back and forth in front of their eyes, and that it was only due to bad luck that they hadn't found either on one of their random vehicle checks.

This had been explained to Ken and he liked to go on about it, how brilliant it was. He'd been told it was a carny shell game and he loved the expression.

The shell game, however, was merely a ruse. The intention was to keep the cops focused on the vehicles, trying to discern which were in play, while the drugs were actually being moved in another manner altogether. Most of the people, and all of the supplies and product, travelled through the woods. They were snuck in and out of the lab through a trap door hidden among some trees.

Detective Swain, trailing the swat team, had first gone to the farmhouse and discovered that no one was at home except a biker pretending to watch TV. They looked around, but nothing of any evidentiary value was found.

Swain then trudged down to the barn, past the intimidation and racket of the German Shepherd that caused him to briefly consider shooting the damn thing in the head.

Instead, he spoke in a normal tone to it, expecting the dog to calm, but it snarled in return. Just as well that he couldn't justify killing a chained animal, he thought, it wasn't the dog's fault it was mean. It had undoubtedly been trained to be that way.

Swain was met just inside the barn by one Sergeant Welty and given a quick tour. The two bikers they passed were sitting placidly on lawn chairs just inside the door, like guests at a community barbecue. They called out "Hi" to the police in an exceedingly friendly way.

Swain had no interest in the men; just the barn. He poked his head into a revolting little bathroom consisting of a grungy sink and a toilet with its seat down, covered in piss, and felt a surge of disgust.

"Have a look over here," said the sergeant, pointing to a metal door.

Swain poked his head through the doorway. The confined, windowless space was lit by a single hanging bulb. The only thing in a room, which measured something like three metres by two, was a metal-framed single bed with a ratty mattress.

"Looks like some sort of confinement room," said Swain's companion.

"I like to crash here sometimes," chimed up one of the lawn chair farmers.

"Save it sonny boy," said Swain who remained standing at the doorway of the room, considering, then deciding eventually, that there was nothing that could be done about the existence of the chamber, however suspicious it was.

After a half hour search, Swain and his team left the premises. No needle found among the haystacks; nothing of anything else either. For four months they'd had the farm under surveillance, waiting for this day. Their intelligence told them there was a lab on the farm that was up and running for weeks at a time, and that this was one of those weeks. But they'd found nothing. It suggested their intelligence was wrong because a drug lab isn't easy to hide, especially not one on the reputed scale they were looking for. There would have to be plumbing and ventilation, shelves of chemicals, bottles, tubing, and more; not to mention people.

That somewhere on the farm there was a hidden entrance, was still Swain's opinion, but he conceded to himself that it might be time to look elsewhere, and forget about the farm.

10.

Tuesday: he did die but he came back

Shortly after the debacle at Grandma's, Louis had parked the car on a side road. He couldn't get a motel room because the credit card found inside the stolen Capri was too hot to use again, and he needed the cash he had for food.

The pair slept until first light then drove to a roadside diner. The place was locally renowned for its vast inventory of black velvet paintings (advertised with a huge flashing sign outside reading, '*Fine Art*'). It also featured an all day breakfast special with bottomless coffee. Louis counted seven different versions of Elvis immortalized on velvet. One more than Jesus.

"So where to now?" Ida asked.

"My brother's."

Drawing her head back as if to gain a better perspective, Ida said, "I thought he died." But she shifted and resumed her position when something occurred to her. "Different brother obviously. I didn't realize you had more than the one."

"No, same one. He did die but he came back. Word from South America was he'd killed himself but it wasn't true; he just showed up back here one day. Surprised the hell outta me."

"How the hell do you get a message saying someone you love is dead when they aren't? That's shocking! I'd sue someone's ass."

"I don't know what happened. My brother doesn't wanna talk about anythin'. Guess it was a different guy who died and Larry wasn't around so they thought it was him. But I don't know, he's changed, not looks-wise, but he seems resentful, like we willed him to come back home, like it was somethin' he had to do and he didn't like it. He seems different with me even though he's always been distant since that stuff when he was a teenager. But he's even more standoffish now."

"What stuff?"

"Didn't I tell ya?"

"I don't know, I don't remember anything about it."

"He went into the hospital one time. I was about twelve. It was set up like a maternity ward. The staff observed people through a glass wall."

"A secure unit in a psych ward!"

"Yeah. I remember my parents left me in there to hang with Larry while they talked to the staff in the nurse's station. We watched them through the glass that surrounded it, having this big discussion. After awhile I wanted to go home so I wandered down there. While I was waiting outside the door I could hear them talkin'. The doctor was sayin' to my parents that he would tell Larry that he had to go to school; that this was not negotiable. Then my parents started spewing this business wisdom crap about teamwork, how we were all on the same team and had to pull together. It was bullshit meant to get the doctor on their side for what they wanted, and that was to keep Larry in the hospital indefinitely. When the doctor said somethin' about discharging Larry, my parents got all worked up and started makin' up stories about bad stuff Larry had done. At the time though, I didn't know they were lies. They called him a 'misfit' and argued that he needed to be institutionalized. They just wanted to be rid of the poor bugger. It was the first time I came across parents lying to hurt their kids, and when I was older and realized what my parents had done it had a big effect on me. The doctor ended up arguin' with my parents, trying to get them to take Larry with them, but they resisted. On the way home, they were rippin' and roarin' about what a crap doctor the guy was."

"So Larry came home with you."

"Not then. My parents went on their way without him. The hospital kept Larry for about two weeks. He was always cold to us after that, like he suspected what my parents were up to. Or maybe it was the medication he was on. You know what it's like; they're always pushin' some kind of crap down your throat, tellin' you that you're sick. I hated it too, startin' with the Ritalin my mother insisted I take, cus I wasn't a zombie doin' exactly what she said. Really fucks you up in a lot of ways; someone insisting you're not normal."

"And you were probably just being an active kid. No

wonder Larry seemed nasty when he came back. Maybe he tried to set up his own disappearance."

Louis hesitated, in earnest contemplation. "Never thought of that."

"Yeah, Scrabble," Louis said while he drove, explaining the dream he'd had during the night. "I was playing Scrabble with Shakespeare and James Joyce. They both kept making up words. Joyce had one word with z, x and q in it. It was worth something like 250 points. They both seemed to think this was okay."

The sun didn't come up that day, plus there was steam on the inside of the car's front window and an opaque film of rainwater on the outside that the wipers were powerless against. Foliage and tree boughs drooped low from the deluge dumped by huge black clouds. Not only did the willows weep but the sumac sobbed, the crabgrass cried, and all sorts of other humanized phenomena occurred.

Louis's voice faded as he rolled down his window to get his bearings from the edge of the road. He'd told Ida when they set off how he liked this sort of weather because it made for a good a respite from the mosquitoes, but he was soon complaining about what a 'bitch' it was to drive with his head hanging out of the window.

"So how have you been?" Ida asked after the rain eased and Louis retracted his head like a turtle who'd seen too much of life.

"Not bad." Louis combed his hair with open fingers and wiped the water from his eyes with the base of his thumb.

"What happened to your van? Did you gamble it away?"

"No, no. Just decided to get a car. Got this one right before I picked up Joseph."

"You working?"

"Here and there."

"Ever consider going back into gardening?"

"Naw."

"But you used to love it!"

"I had enough."

"You had some interesting ideas."

51

"They weren't mine, they mostly came from Alexander Pope. Took him five years to build his garden. Stuff grew wild in the areas where it was put. It was structured wildness. There was no symmetry, trimmed trees, or straight paths. But no one likes that style anymore. Pope is definitely not hip. If I was to work in the business now it'd just be all garden beds in patterns. Routine, boring crap. Not like I was doing much work that was interesting, even when I had the business. It was pretty low level and the same sort of gardens, day in, day out."

"Okay, but still, you were running your own successful business. That's not low level."

"Yeah, I guess. In some ways I was glad when it got shuttered, but I was still pissed cus it wasn't my fault it went belly up. I was workin' almost full time for a developer named Garcia and the bastard went out of business owing me a lot of money. He built a slew of buildings and then went bankrupt. His son Alex was okay, paid me on time, but old man Garcia was a crook. People used to tell me not to do business with a Uruguayan, you know how you hear that, but I don't buy it, I'm not prejudiced. They're no more crooked than anyone else. But old man Garcia was doing his best to make sure that old stereotypes don't die… Son of a bitch."

Ida said nothing, reflecting critically on the story. Amongst what sort of people exactly did one find Uruguayan stereotypes? And it seemed to her that there was reason to doubt Louie's claim of not being a racist. He had once been part of a heavy metal band in his youth and he'd told her that he used to dress like a skinhead. But maybe that was more like a costume, she thought, instantly defending him. That would make sense. Louis had once told her how one night, just before the band was to perform, that he'd noticed a bunch of people dressed just like him, so he went home, lost his facial hardware and outfit, and put on a suit for the performance. Afterwards, that became his performing wardrobe, and once he was really famous – according to Louis's version of history, anyway – a lot of his admirers dressed in suits in the hope of subsuming Louis Henderson's identity. Everyone it seemed was lost and wanting to pick up an identity on the cheap.

Ida hadn't researched this. She didn't like metal music, not that she'd say so to Louis, and the one time she had looked up a song he mentioned, she couldn't find either a video or lyrics anywhere on the internet.

"I didn't declare bankruptcy," Louis continued, revving himself back up. "Everybody said to. I owed a fuck of a lot for plants and supplies, but I didn't want to screw over nobody like old Garcia screwed me. Uruguayan bastard."

After this flash fire of resentment sputtered out, Louis was fine. Ten years he'd run the business and there hadn't been time for anything else. And what was just as bad was that, for all his efforts, he could never afford anything new. Old car, old clothes, old furniture, old TV, old face, old hands, old solitude. Not having the business wasn't such a bad thing.

"I needed a break from responsibility," he said.

Ida hesitated. Dwelling on this comment would only annoy her.

After two hours of driving, our intrepid heroes passed through the village of New Coppermine. It was a typical northern town; a dozen or so diminutive wooden houses facing the highway, five newish places behind them on the town's lone street (constituting a rural northern version of the suburb) and of course, a Catholic church.

As Louis slowed the car, he announced to a dozing Ida, "We're here."

He turned right, just past the last of the village houses, onto a dirt road that he followed for maybe five hundred metres before turning left onto a narrow 'driveway' (i.e. two curving grooves worn into overgrown grass) for a hundred metres or so before parking in front of a low to the ground wooden bungalow constructed of drab grey barn board. The place seemed even more squat than it actually was because there was no visible foundation and the high grass reduced the discernible walls to something like a metre and a half. The parking area was just a bit of flattened grass between the end of the drive and the garage, which was attached to the house. They pulled up beside a parked Mazda pick-up truck.

Ida, did a quick, fatal assessment of the place, got hesitantly out of the car and retrieved her bag from the trunk. Her face muscles slowly relaxed as she rationalized to herself that, after all, they were only staying here for a few days.

"Hey bro!" shouted Louis when they got to the screen door. The inner door was open and he walked in.

Ida followed. The taut springs on the screen door caused it to nail her ass.

It was a sparsely furnished room, she noted. Worn but spotless. Not what she would have expected in a man's place.

The two intruders walked to the centre of the room without removing their shoes and stood in front of a small coffee table, the likes of which neither had seen for thirty years.

"Hey there's the man!" Louis said with affection. "Ida, this is Larry," he continued, waving his hand in the general direction of a man slouching against the far wall, beside the bedroom door.

The guy was tall with slim arms folded across his chest, and rolled up sleeves. He nodded in Ida's direction. There was no change to his indifferent expression.

"Hi! Nice to meet you," Ida said brightly. Was Larry upset? she wondered. He certainly appeared to be pissed off. She glanced at Louis for assurance and then back to the immutable Larry. She looked desperately towards the door.

"Great to see you," Louis said to his brother and, though he stepped forward, he didn't go near him or offer his hand. "Hope you don't mind. Thought we'd drop in for a few days and go fishing in the Lethe."

Larry didn't react. He looked to be pinned against the wall, like a butterfly to a board, and his expression suggested this was the only thing preventing him from retreating entirely.

"Power corrupts. Money corrupts," said Larry in a thin tinny voice.

Ida looked back and forth between Larry and Louis, bewildered.

"Yeah, absolutely," said Louis with a smile, obviously aware of the routine.

"Secrecy increases in such environments," added Larry.

"Righto," said Louis.

Ida forced a smile in Larry's direction, as if he'd said something hospitable. She glanced at the bag in her hand.

"Sorry if we're inconveniencing you," she said politely. "If we are, don't be afraid to say so, and we'll go."

Larry said nothing.

"We're family," Louis said to Ida, meaning, 'put away your concerns'.

There was something very familiar about Larry's appearance, Ida thought, but she couldn't say why since she was fairly certain she'd never met him before. Since Larry continued to look down at the floor, Ida continued to stare at him. The word 'disoriented' came to mind but then, almost immediately, it occurred to her that maybe Larry was merely trying to give her that impression so she would be afraid of him and urge Louie to leave. Craziness can be quite sane.

11.

off to the Indian Wars

Two hours later, the man that Louis referred to as Larry (but who otherwise went by the name of Lawrence) stopped his nearly new Mazda pick-up on the gravel shoulder of the highway, a good ways before the driveway leading to Reg's farm.

Reg Phelps – a young man with luxuriant red hair – was waiting, and looking nervously up and down the road. He had asked that pick-ups and drop-offs be at this spot because he didn't like his father to know who he was with. Here, he couldn't be seen from the house. The old man was strict, a cop, saw his son as cowardly and untrustworthy, and wanted to keep him out of trouble.

Reg was afraid of the old guy. Felt he would never be beyond his fear of him. He was sure that his old man would become violent if he knew of the physical relationship he shared with Lawrence. Even if the sex wasn't an issue the fact of Lawrence's age – about fifty – would be.

Reg and Lawrence weren't a couple because they loved each other, but because they were both lonely, trapped inside their own worlds. There were no other men that either was close to.

Not having to interact with Reg's old man suited Lawrence fine. He didn't like dealing with people any more than he needed to.

Reg, carrying a backpack and hatchet, and looking like he was off to the Indian Wars, jumped in the truck. He was always ready for a run to the reserve that straddled the U.S. border, for tax-free cigarettes; and Lawrence appreciated his willingness. The fact that Reg didn't say much en route, and then always did the negotiating and interacting when they got there, made him the perfect partner.

The two men had come back from a trip to the reservation the day before, so this run didn't fit the usual schedule. Such spontaneity was quite unlike Lawrence, but he had needed to get away from Louis. He was instantly miserable when the guy showed up, and this time Louis had brought a woman with him. Lawrence felt no connection whatsoever to Louis. He just wanted the guy to leave him alone.

"Hey Lawrence," Reg said. "See you finally cleaned the truck."

This was meant as a joke but Lawrence merely looked confused. The cleanliness of his truck was always meticulously maintained.

"Wasn't expecting you to call," Reg said, "but I'm glad you did. The old man is in a pissy mood. Buggin' me about getting' a job. Called me a 'prince', like I think work is beneath me. I says to him, 'And who were the three wise men at **your** birth?' He didn't like that much, gettin' his own back, but he had it comin'."

No response. Lawrence usually ignored him, which Reg took for simply being taciturn.

"We need to purchase some green garbage bags before we get to the reserve," Lawrence said. "Remind me will you, please?"

"Sure, no problem," answered a grinning Reg. To his ear, everything his partner said sounded stilted and overly formal. The guy had been some sort of professor people said. Or maybe it was a processor, whatever the fuck that was. Some said, he was a teacher. There were all kinds of competing stories. Lawrence wouldn't answer Reg's questions about such things, so there was no way of sorting them out.

"You can sleep till we get there," Lawrence said.

"Naw, I'm not really tired." It was dark because of the weather but it was still just midday.

Reg flicked on the radio and began to twist the dial. "We need some tunes," he said brightly, snapping his fingers like he was jivin' in a fifties musical.

12.

sackcloth and ashes

Louis and Ida didn't go fishing in the afternoon because a show-stopping deluge of rain was again pounding down. Instead, they lay on the couch together and napped. After that they rooted around in the cupboards, and opened and ate a couple of tins of canned spaghetti. Louis found some Canadian Club above the fridge, a large, half-filled bottle, and the pair started in on it.

They watched TV on a small ancient set. There was only one channel. Louis would have preferred a cop show, one of those with sexy settings and actors, set in Hawaii or Florida, but an entertainment tabloid show was on instead. An actress was crying, apologizing to the 'public' for some sexual indiscretion, as if the public had been offended. Mea culpa. Sackcloth and ashes. This was ridiculous, Louis thought. He had no interest in public shaming, and had always been bewildered by this odd notion that the body public had a say over one's sex life.

"I have an idea for an invention," Louis said, as they watched.

"What's that?"

"Something that you could aim at the screen. I don't know the technology but – just so you get the idea of what I mean – think of it as a laser pointer. When you point it at the screen, an information box pops up. What's in the box depends on where you point. So you know how you might say, 'I wonder where I've seen that actor before?', you could point at the guy, click, and you'd get his list of credits."

"Don't they have something like that?"

"I don't know. Don't think so."

The two sat in silence for a minute or so, watching.

"What about you? Ya got any genius ideas?" Louis said.

"Yes I do, me and Sally actually…greeting cards. You know how you would make your parents cards when you were a kid? We'd make hand-made cards that look like those, only call them art cards."

58

"Nice."

They soon gave up on the TV and for the next three hours drank the remainder of the rye while they played euchre.

Ida eventually threw in her cards and slid back her chair. She shut her eyes and covered them with the spread fingers of her right hand. She slowly brought her fingers together until she was squeezing the bridge of her nose then, sighing, arose and went to the front window where she peered out into the pitch. There was just enough light to discern the contours of the ruts in the grass where the truck had been. "Where did you say Larry went?" she asked.

"I didn't say because I don't know." Louis crossed the room to stand behind her. "He took off when we were napping. He always does that. We won't see him again 'til the next time we're here."

"He just disappears when you show up?"

"Yep."

"No wonder he looked pissed off. We're putting him out of his house."

"It's his choice. If he doesn't like it, all he has to do is say so and we'll go somewhere else."

They both stared out into the night.

"So where do we sleep?" Ida asked.

"In Larry's bedroom."

Ida turned and smiled seductively. She moved close to Louis until their faces were an inch apart. She slid her hand down the front of his shirt, eventually cupping it under his privates and gently squeezed.

Louis looked into her eyes, reached down, took her free hand and led her into the bedroom.

13.

trying to wash clean his sorry soul

Keith – Ida's sorta boyfriend – walked along the edge of County Road 18. It was an asphalt road that began in front of his apartment, on the edge of the city, and ran south through the countryside.

He couldn't get the accusation made by one of his neighbours out of his head, that the late Stone Cutter had been connected to the local biker gang that was reputed to be the source of a lot of the illegal drugs circulating in the city. And in this part of the world, it was common knowledge, that the gang were in business with the restaurateur Jack Hayes.

Rain, driven westward by a fierce wind, was teeming and had thoroughly soaked Keith's pants from the knees down and the brim of his Mac's ball cap. They were the only parts of him that his raincoat didn't cover. He stayed on the right shoulder of the road, frequently looking up ahead, where, in the distance, the ghostly silhouette of the roof of Jack Hayes's barn was visible beyond the fields.

Inside Keith's backpack was a high-powered set of binoculars, purchased that morning, but he didn't remove them. Their intended purpose was to allow him, at long last, to satisfy his curiosity about this hive of old-style gangsters – as he imagined the place – without any risk of being seen.

Suddenly, pushing all hesitation aside, Keith drew a deep breath and veered down through the ditch. It was an act he'd been contemplating as he walked, but had repeatedly rejected; his justifications covering up his lack of nerve.

Climbing over the wire fence, on the other side of the ditch, Keith avoided the barbed top strand by hanging on to a 'No Trespassing' sign attached to it. He fell face first into a cow pasture, his ball cap knocked down over his eyes.

By sheer luck, Keith had picked for his place of egress, one of the few spots along the fence that Hayes's security cameras didn't cover; their view of that spot being blocked by a huge tree. Because of that, the sleepy biker in the farmhouse office, named Jeb, who was watching the TV security monitors (while putting back his sixth beer of the night) didn't register the trespasser.

Keith picked his way across the field. After negotiating his way over another barbed wire fence, he discovered that making his way through the bush he now found himself in was a bigger challenge than the field. On the ground were boulders of various sizes, tossed there over the years to clear the field for tilling. It was treacherous going in the rain and dark. Keith stumbled over an unseen obstacle and fell on a large rock that connected with his stomach, like a good left jab, leaving him momentarily winded and sapped of strength.

Unbeknownst to Keith, ahead in the underground bunker below the barn, a group of bikers were celebrating the day's unsuccessful police raid. They were playing poker, sitting around the table in the lab. They could have played in the barn loft but knew that Jaycee – Jack Hayes' girlfriend – would see the light and rat them out to Jack. His rule was 'no lights in the loft after dark', lest the watching cops spot them.

As was his wont, Kenny was earnestly putting back more beers than anyone else; nine by last count. It was a source of profound personal pride that he could not be drunk under the table by anyone. "Goin' to take a leak," he announced suddenly, got up and headed, not for the bathroom but down the tunnel towards the trap door and the bush.

"You know it's pissing rain out there, don't cha?" asked one of his cronies.

"I like the fresh air."

"Fresh air? That's like saying you'll get fresh air at the bottom of a lake," said Lemony.

A chuckle went around, but Kenny ignored it. He managed to avoid staggering, attempting to maintain the image he liked to project, of invincibility in the face of alcohol, but once away from the scrutiny of the other bikers, he allowed himself the pleasure of reeling a bit and bouncing lightly off the tunnel walls. At the end of the tunnel he climbed the ladder and, with great difficulty, raised the trapdoor above his head until it flopped over. It weighed in the area of twenty kilos because attached to it was four centimetres of cement, painted to look like dirt, and inserted into the concrete was a variety of fake shrubbery to help it blend into the surroundings.

"Bitch!" he cursed at the door. "Bitch," he said again on first being showered by the rain. It was ferociously pelting down as if trying to wash clean his sorry soul. That would have been a thankless effort.

Kenny climbed out of the tunnel and tried to make a drunken run for the shelter of some nearby trees but caught his toe on a small, half buried rock. He went over in drunken slow motion, arms at his side, like timber falling, his forehead colliding with a boulder that knocked him into a semi-conscious stupor, one step below his usual cognitive state. Blood began to ooze over his face.

In his short but eventful time outside, Kenny hadn't noticed the figure approaching through the trees.

And Keith hadn't seen Kenny either. When he first stepped around a tree to be confronted with the outline of the prone biker on the ground, Keith took root and stared open mouthed. The guy was just visible enough, from the diffused light coming from the open tunnel door, to see that his face was soaked in blood. Keith shuddered with excitement at what he took to be a murdered man. All his dreams of what an actual criminal lair might look like had seemingly come to fruition.

The sound of laughing voices in the tunnel caused him to raise his head. The look of horror on his face indicated he was expecting to see someone emerge.

Spinning, and beginning to flee, he went face first into the first tree he came to. A low hanging brach skimmed the top of his head knocking back the hood of his raincoat. His Mac's Trucking ball cap was sent flying behind him.

He reeled backwards. After regaining his balance, he set off through the bush, leaving his cap behind. He leaped over the fence without so much as touching it, and landed on his stomach in the field.

Fortunately for Keith the rain was letting up, making this trip over the field marginally easier than his first one. He galloped and stumbled through the ruts, but tore his arm and jacket going over the roadside fence. Back on the road he

62

began to sprint. The city limits were about a kilometre up the county road, and in spite of the fact he was out of shape and his guts were wracked with pain as he sucked in air, Keith managed the kilometre in six minutes and nineteen seconds without stopping to rest.

"What happened to Kenny?" one of the poker players eventually queried.

"Bet the fucker passed out," laughed Wayne. It had been twenty minutes since Kenny had left.

"Probably purgating," said another.

"Purgating?" asked Lemony.

"Yeah. Pur-gate-ing."

Everyone let it go, as if that was clarification.

"Let me check on him," said Lemony and headed up the tunnel. He stepped over the puddle of rainwater at the bottom of the ladder, climbed a few rungs, and paused with his head slightly above ground level while his eyes adjusted. The rain had stopped but the night was still impenetrable. Soon, due to the light escaping the tunnel entrance, he could make out Kenny struggling to stand up, bent at the waist, knees wobbling.

Lemony climbed out, went to his friend, and took his arm to support him. "You okay bro?"

"Don' know Lemon Man." Kenny's mumbling was almost incoherent.

"What the fuck's all this blood on your face?"

"I fell, I think."

"Yeah, no shit." Lemony picked up the black ball cap laying on the ground and put it on Kenny's head before slipping his hand under the guy's armpit to help him back to the tunnel.

Kenny, swiping with his free hand, knocked the offending cap to the ground.

Back at his apartment, after catching his breath, Keith called Crime Stoppers.

"Yeah, I want to report a murder," he said coolly, affecting his most sinister tone of voice. "You'll find the prick laying in the bush back of the barn at Jack Hayes's farm, in a clearing. I'm sure you'll know who he is and if not, check with your Gangs Taskforce."

Keith had made no conscious decision beforehand to imply that he was involved in the events he was reporting. It was just that the longing to be a gangster, always intense, always wanting to overpower his dull life, saw its chance, reached out and took hold. Not willing to hang up, Keith described the exact location of the corpse relative to the barn and, this time, referred to the body as 'that bastard'. He struggled against the urge to give his name and glowed with happiness when he hung up at this sense of being on the inside, and of spilling the dope to the cops as if he was involved. He was a mobster rock star.

Keith went to the window and stared out. His rundown apartment building was one of a cluster near the edge of the city. It was a sort of refugee camp for exiles (the poor, aged, and those excluded from having a stake in society). He was usually an intense watcher of the life outside – it was the closest thing to human interaction that many of the atomized residents ever experienced – but tonight he took nothing in. Tonight he was a participant in life – it was crime's gift – and he was consumed with thoughts of the tunnel he'd seen. It had to be a secret entrance to something. But what?

He grabbed hold of his insider information and clutched it to his wannabe gangster heart. There was no way he was going to relinquish it by sharing it with the cops. "God," he prayed aloud to the deity of tunnels, "Please don't let the cops find it."

An hour later, five police cars stopped at the gate of the Hayes farm, initiating the second internal alarm in sixteen hours. This time, the cops ignored the house and drove directly to the barn.

Inside it, a repeat of the biker's ritual was being enacted. The vertical section of the tunnel received its waterproof false bottom, half way down, buckets of water were dumped into the hole, a section of fencing was extracted and cows were shooed into an extension of their pen.

But the cops weren't interested in tunnels. They fanned out around the back of the barn with a sergeant shouting orders.

Looking from her bedroom window, Jaycee saw the ghostly apparitions of glistening ponchos floating in a crazy dance around the side of the barn, the orange glow from flashlights bobbing in and out of sight.

Jack still wasn't home from the hospital so she took responsibility for settling the matter herself. She was soon downstairs and through the kitchen door, while still wrapping a coat around herself.

In the middle of the yard she approached Detective Swain who was on his way to the house. When they were three metres apart, in a voice loud enough to be heard over the ruckus from the riled up German Shepherd, the detective began to explain the purpose of the visit.

As they came face to face, Jaycee screamed, "Like I give a fuck what some lying bastard caller said. Like I believe someone even called. I am ordering you to get off of the property. Immediately!"

She was advised by the detective, speaking in a bored but businesslike voice, that they would leave after concluding their investigation, that they had reasonable cause to be here, and that, in the meantime, that she should return to the house or risk being charged with obstruction.

Aware of the ways of police when it came to bikers, but not until after unloading several more curses and threats, Jaycee went back to the house, yelling back that her next act would be to call her lawyer.

Swain returned to the barn, grateful for the presence of the nearby cops because the truth was that he was nervous in the dark. He smiled conspiratorially at an officer he passed who smirked back at him.

"That's one classy broad," said Swain, getting a laugh in return.

"Over here! Over here!" yelled a cop from behind the barn, standing beside a large rock with bloody rivulets and puddles on it.

Sergeant Quick went to investigate and called his people together. Notified by radio, Swain joined the assembly to find

Quick flinging out orders, all the while jabbing his finger in different directions.

Since no one had been looking for a tunnel entrance, none was found, but neither was a dead body. A bloody rock had been spotted, however, and Quick – ironically standing on the cover to the drug lab tunnel – made sure that the evidence was immediately protected in case the rain resumed. The search for a body, his people were told, should continue around him and be done without damaging the scene.

Quick sneezed and vigorously rubbed the inside of his ear with a forefinger. "Fucking allergies," he cursed as the officers again spread out. Almost immediately, one of the men called out, "There's a baseball cap here Sergeant."

Quick and Swain made their way over. "Here," said a young officer, shining a light on his find. The two men in charge bent over to have a look. They saw a black cap, right side up, sitting under the tree. It had a Mac's Trucking crest on the front.

One of the officers, Beatty was his name, looked perplexed but said nothing. There was something about that crest on the cap.

"Bag it quick!" directed the sergeant, "before the rain starts up again."

"If there ever was a body," Swain said, as much to himself as to Quick, "it's gone now."

"Detective," Constable Beatty said to Swain. "Sorry to interrupt sir, but there's something I should mention." He began by telling Swain about the apartment he'd gone to that week with Detective Rose. A murder scene. The building Superintendent had told them about a baseball cap that was missing from that residence, a Mac's Trucking cap that Stonewall Cutter always wore: the kid who'd been thrown off a balcony.

14.

Wednesday: Keith woke from his possum sleep and his possum dreams

Keith had long ago perfected the strutting attitude of the violent criminal he imagined himself to be. Unlike the rest of his existence, which was purely vicarious, there was an element of truth in this characterization, although the violence in his life was actually just a no holds barred refusal to play along. He was aggressive only when going in the opposite direction to everyone else. And it had been like that for a long time.

At age fourteen, in high school, Keith became an object of ridicule to his classmates, for no obvious reason, but once these sorts of characterizations are made (he was called 'deviant' and 'criminal') they take on a life of their own.

After unsuccessfully objecting to the bullying for a year, Keith reversed course and did his best to embrace the negative characterizations. He would be the criminal outsider, the loner, but of a particular sort – one not immediately evident to those around him. In Keith's mind, the outsider was invested with a certain nobility and morality.

Perhaps he took this route to rescue his self-esteem by pretending that he had chosen his oddness. A rejection of rejection by embracing it.

In any case, he began to wear unusual clothes and to express outrageous attitudes in class, like expounding on the 'beauty of violence'. He loved the thought that he was exuding an aura that induced fear. Of course, this led to further ridicule, but now from a distance.

The whole thing might have eventually worn itself out but one day the principal and a teacher shoved an out of control grade eleven student into the boy's ground floor washroom and locked the door to wait for the kid to calm down. Keith, who had witnessed the incident, went outside to where some grounds work was going on, and grabbed a huge sledgehammer he'd seen earlier. He took out the washroom window with one fierce swing, even half the frame, and was making good headway on the wall when collared by the cops. The trapped student was found cowering in a stall, not grasping that Keith was trying to liberate him.

No charges were laid against Keith because the principal successfully argued for psychiatric care instead.

When Keith resumed his education he was completely avoided by every teenager in the school – to his delight. He was now an actual criminal so he no longer had to deal with taunting, even from a distance.

His psychiatrist suggested that he was very lonely and wanted to be in a gang for the sense of camaraderie. Keith stopped seeing the guy. He wasn't lonely, he thought, and he didn't need pals. He just wanted excitement and for people to look up to him. If it came in the form of his being in an imaginary gang, that was fine with him.

Once he was older and out on his own, physical relationships, like the one with Ida, provided some degree of comfort but even that was something that he could live without. The relationship with Ida was just sex, at least for Keith. Fucking was a verb, adjective and even a noun in Fucking, Austria. It was everything and nothing. Everything to some; nothing to him.

Shortly before eight AM, Keith awoke from his possum sleep and his possum dreams and immediately staged breakfast on his IKEA dining set – juice, coffee and cereal – and turned on the TV morning news. He wanted everything to be just right for when the announcer eventually reported that a body had been found at the Hayes farm, thanks to an anonymous tip. He wanted to take in the report without reaction, like some hardened mob boss, like it was a commonplace that there would be mention in the media of a crime he was connected to.

He sat, ate and listened. The usual political figures and issues were mentioned. The usual crimes were described – plus a monkey was running loose downtown – but nothing about a body in a field.

In spite of himself Keith got up and began to pace with fists clenched. Addressing the screen he said, "What the fuck's the matter with you guys?" He picked up the TV

68

remote to change the channel to a more reputable station, one that wasn't filled with the insignificant, one that would know the import of a dead gangster in a field, but he felt that as soon as he did so he would miss news about the man's body.

Time ticked down. With about fifteen seconds left in the show, the useless announcer read that a known biker with connections to organized crime – one Lawrence (Lemony) Boissoneault – had been named as a 'person of interest' in the death of Stonewall Cutter. The police were now treating it as a murder. The latter name didn't immediately mean anything to Keith, hearing it in a new context, but it eventually struck him that this was the name of the kid who had died in his building.

So, he thought, the kid's death was a murder after all. The wannabe gangster, was overcome by a tidal surge of jealousy because this news meant that the kid really had been involved with local bikers, so likely those working with Hayes – while he wasn't.

Keith struggled to keep his head above the raging emotional waters that made it hard to take in the picture of Lemony that was flashed up on the screen. The angular features, the aquiline nose, the Viking long blonde hair.

Keith signed on to his computer after the frustrating newscast to check fruitlessly for news of a body, but eventually, once he'd calmed down, he found a good photo of Lemony.

He knew in his gut where Lemony was at this moment – somewhere down the tunnel under the Hayes barn.

Keith went to the window to stare out, unfocused, towards the distant horizon, as if making some cosmic linkage with the world's mobster mamas' boys. Keith re-affirmed his decision not to call and inform the cops about the tunnel. If he did there would be no information left that was just his. Had he given the right location of the body to them, he wondered? Had they even searched for it? He knew that somehow he was going to have to show them what a mistake they'd made.

69

15.

the River Lethe

"I thought you said this was the River Lethe," Ida said, as Louis pulled the Capri to a stop amid metre-high grass at the side of a creek. They'd driven a hundred metres along some overgrown ruts running through the trees. "The sign on the highway says '*Little Creek*'."

"It was a joke," Louis said. "Larry calls the creek 'Lethe'; it comes from Greek mythology. Lethe is the spirit who washes away memories. She's a daughter of the God of strife, sister of the deities of toil, starvation, pain, fights, and lies. So she sorta cleans up after her siblings I guess you could say."

"Okay," Ida said dubiously, not getting the joke. "You got things you want to forget?"

"Don't we all?"

"I guess. So you going to be taking a swim to wash off?"

"Not me. I'm too old for that stuff." Louis missed more than a few jokes himself. "When we were kids we'd jump in, even in the spring when it was freezin' cold, but not anymore."

Louis had been pulling gear out of the trunk while they talked. He opened a bottle of bug repellent, splashed some onto his palm, and passed the bottle to Ida. Once they had slathered that around their exposed parts, Louis opened the bottle filled with the worms he'd dug up earlier. He handed out the fishing rods, showed Ida how to hold hers, and put a worm on each of their hooks, all the while maintaining a running pedagogical dialogue.

"So you used to come here?" Ida said when there was a break in the lesson.

"My old man would bring us. Once, when I was about twelve, I found a guy on the bank up stream layin' there with an axe in his back." He waved in the general direction.

"Fuck!" Ida looked incredulous. "That must have affected you."

"Naw. Stuff like that doesn't bother kids much. But you remember it."

"No wonder there's stuff you want to forget."

The pair climbed down the bank, through abundant purple loosestrife which was proliferating, squeezing out the other plants for soil. In the social relations of the field it was top dog, commanding every resource.

The waters of the Lethe slid sensually by, seductively caressing the boulders that protruded above the surface. Louis and Ida jumped to a large flat rock in the river, and began moving from rock to rock, sometimes leaping, and sometimes stepping into the cold creek to avoid travelling the banks which were too crowded with vegetation to walk on.

Speckled trout were the only type of fish that they caught. The fishers stopped and worked every pool of deep still water that had developed in the shelter of the large boulders. Louis, calling the shots, directed Ida about when to stop and when to move on.

Ida soon lost her enthusiasm for fishing and Louis was too absorbed in manipulating his rod up and down to notice. He frequently hooked small fish and let them loose while Ida caught nothing. She would dip her line into the creek in a way that all but told the fish to avoid it. They obeyed, teasingly nibbling at her worm till there was nothing left of it. She continued to fish after that, pointlessly, with a blank hook rather than skewer another worm. Louis had solemnly told her that she ought to put worms on her hook herself, like this was a life skill she needed to master, 'teach a woman to fish etc' he lectured, as if she would ever need to catch fish herself to survive.

Ida had no interest in the fish end of the business.

It wasn't that she wasn't enjoying herself, on the contrary, she was absorbed with the experience of being in the country, thrilled with the wind's touch, with the lift and swoon of the branches overhead, and the multitude of sounds. She plucked leaves from overhanging branches, dropped them in the water and watched them flow and eddy aimlessly like so many lives.

"I think I'll call Sally when we get back," she said at one point. "Find out if she got the job."

"Isn't that a foregone conclusion?"

"Likely. But I'd still like to know for sure."

Louis didn't answer, yanking his hook to the surface along with a fish.

"So you like this?" he asked.

"It's wonderful, but there's lots of bugs, even with the bug repellent... I thought we'd be going in a boat."

"Sorry. Boats cost money and I don't think my brother has much."

"That's fine. I wasn't complaining... What's he do for a living?"

Louis snickered. "Fucked if I know. We don't talk much. I sorta gave up tryin'. It's like he's mute. He used to be a tailor but I can't see him doin' that around here."

"No, that's a pretty small town he lives near. Maybe he's happy though, doing whatever it is he's doing. His place isn't great but he's obviously getting by."

"I wonder sometimes if he's involved in somethin' illegal."

"Like what?"

"I don't know."

Ida looked at him but Louis's face communicated nothing about how the remark was meant. "Seriously?"

"No," Louis laughed. "Not really. He's not like me. Let's move on." He meant this in multiple ways, pulling his hook out of the water and jumping to a new rock.

Ida followed. She didn't react to Louis's comment regarding his familiarity with crime. He'd told her the details of a litany of crimes he'd committed in his youth and she superstitiously felt that not talking about these things was the best way to keep that sort of behaviour in the past. Out of sight, out of mind.

Louis stopped abruptly, balancing on a nearly pointed stone he'd just leapt to, turned towards Ida, and said, "You had enough?"

"Yeah."

They reversed their route. Because they were no longer fishing, the trip back up the river took only fifteen minutes.

As they climbed the bank, Louis, with studied casualness, said, "You ever contemplate doin' anything illegal? I don't mean like runnin' a red light or somethin' but committing a real crime."

Ida stopped as if struck by a fist to the face and stared at him for several seconds, then snorted and vigorously shook her head. "Fuck! I knew it!" she swore. "I knew the minute you called me that you had something in mind. Are you that broke? Is that it? I figured you must be since you don't have your business anymore and we're stealing food from your brother. You could try getting a job like everyone else."

"They're hard to come by. You know that."

"What is it? What do you want me to help you with? Rob another one of your relatives? Fuck off Louie, I won't do it!"

"I was thinking more like a bank."

"Phew," she exhaled loudly. "Sure! Why not? A bank. Are you fucking crazy?"

The question went unanswered for a few moments as they finished climbing the embankment and returned to the Capri. Louis began to pack things into the trunk while Ida stood off to the side.

"You bastard," Ida said softly, "I thought for a minute there you actually wanted to be with me."

"I do. Course I do, but when we were drivin' along you were tellin' me how you couldn't get a job and would have to sleep with someone to get one…"

"A joke!"

"Yeah, I know. But it made me think of this bank near here. I think a big score is somethin' that'll help both of us."

"Then go for it…but after you take me home."

"I can't do it alone."

Ida got in to the car and slammed the door. "Whatever," she said aloud. Louie's suggestion was repulsive and miles out of her realm of experience. I don't have to do anything I don't want to, she told herself.

Louis dallied outside. He always felt guilty lying. He'd intended to make this proposal to Ida from the beginning. To him, everyone fit into some sort of stereotype, and he thought of Ida as the poor and manipulatable sort. The robbery, he'd told himself, would help her.

As she waited, Ida's mood turned to anger. She had come

on the trip to spend time with Louis and now she realized that he'd only invited her because he wanted help with a crime. It reminded her of every humiliation of the last few years. Things always turned out the same with men. "You get treated like this because you let them," Sally had once said. "You'd be better off with the old guys at work who're always hitting on you. At least then you'd get a meal and a movie out of the deal." It was only partially a joke.

Louis eventually joined Ida in the car and swung himself sideways, hooking a knee over the stick shift. "Wait till you hear what I gotta say. Give me a chance to explain."

"Save your breath. It's crazy." Ida's voice was hard and devoid of all inflection. "You're not talking me into this."

"Would it hurt to listen?"

"It could."

"No it won't. Is your life so wonderful? You're broke, you can't even find a minimum wage job, you might lose your apartment. You can't tell me you saved any money with what you were makin'. I'm just thinkin' 'bout you. You deserve better. With a few grand you might be able to start that greeting card business. Maybe take that vacation with Sally."

Ida said nothing. Sure, she thought, Louis came up with the idea of robbing a bank for her benefit. Now he was assuming she was stupid enough to buy this bull. Did the insults never end?

Louis straightened up, started the car, and steered it back to the road.

Ida thought about the time, several months before, when she had applied for a loan to start a business. It was a no go because she'd been a good girl and paid with cash through the years. The bank's credit check was yet one more humiliation. It was like they had the power to determine if you existed. I have a credit history, therefore I am. To be a real person you had to have a past of paid off loans and credit cards. If not, if you hadn't gotten drawn into the system, you were a non-person.

Louis took her silence to mean she was relenting, so pursued the sympathy line. "I want what's best for you. Life has turned out lousy for both of us. We work our asses off and get nowhere. What I'm thinkin' of is just to get a little somethin' back. Somethin' for us. I've been engaging in a bit of larceny lately and the old skills never go away. I was thinkin' while we were driving – honestly, the idea only came to me yesterday – I was remem'rin' a place near here, a bank that's a little old-fashioned and doesn't look like it has the new security features. I was there a few months ago. They don't even have a guard on duty. I don't think anyone has ever robbed it. It'll be a piece of cake. I know the idea is scary – it scares me too – but if there was ever a chance to make some easy money without gettin' caught, this is it."

"Sounds great. Go for it."

"I'd do it myself and give you half the score but I can't guard the people and scoop the money too."

"So we walk in, take the money and leave? Fuck. That's crazy." Ida wasn't relenting, just resorting to logic.

"Why?"

"Why? Can you hear yourself? What kind of stupid question is that? Cus we'd get caught!"

"I don't think so. But if we do, I'll say I forced you to help. It's a no lose proposition for you. I already thought about that. I'll be the only one with a gun and I'll do the talkin'. You'll just be the one stuffin' money into a bag."

"A gun? Jesus Christ! You have a gun?"

"I have it in my bag. I've had it for years, for protection."

"Geez. So you're going to go into a bank with a gun, get some money and then what? Just walk out?"

"Of course. We walk out and we drive away."

"Of course. Just like that." Ida snorted.

"Yeah. Just like that. I'll steal a car ahead of time and then hide it in the bush for the getaway. You pick me up at that spot and we drive to the bank. Listen, I've thought the whole thing through already. After we rob the bank, we drive this car to where we stashed the other one and switch them. Then I'll get in the trunk and you drive so if a cop goes by they'll see a woman instead of two men and they won't stop you. And you drive towards the town and through it."

"Two men? Where's the other man come in?"

"That's you. I'll get you some clothes and a mask for the

robbery so you can disguise your gender. You can take the disguise off once we get to the place where we switch cars and you take over the driving. Oh, and the new car will be silver, or white or somethin', and the cops'll be lookin' for a purple car. I wonder now if that's why I stole it. So it'll be as memorable as possible. As if I knew ahead of time I was gonna need it for a job."

"What?! You stole this car?" Ida leaned forward in her seat, as if the vehicle was suddenly repulsive.

Louis wore a little boy caught with his hand in the cookie jar kind of shy smile, and said nothing.

"And it's a big purple thing! About the most obvious car on the road. That's how much you think about not getting caught?"

Louis continued looking sheepish. "It's a calculated risk, like everything I do. Don't worry, we won't get caught."

"I'm not worried cus there ain't no 'we'. Have you ever done this before?"

Louis was silent.

"Fucking asshole," Ida murmured.

Nothing more was said during the drive. Ida stared out the window and Louis continually stole nervous glances at her. He hoped she wasn't going to demand to be taken back to the city. But he stifled a grin, immediately replacing it with a serious expression after Ida eventually said in a neutral voice, "And when were you thinking of pulling off this great heist?"

"Today's Wednesday. I thought Friday morning, right after they open. I can't say I know how much money banks usually keep on hand but it'll be payday for a lot of people so I assume that'll be their biggest day cash-wise. The other thing is that, coming up to the weekend, there'll be more cars on the road and that'll mean a lot more cars of likely looking suspects for the cops to pull over. They won't bother stopping you afterwards. Absolutely no way. And anyway, you'll only be drivin' as far as Larry's."

Ida didn't respond. She'd only asked about Louis's plan so she would have all the details when she talked to Sally; when she gave her this example of the sort of colossal, delusional, and self-centred asshole she was hooked up with.

Louis said, "This is a chance to say 'Fuck you, I don't need you' to all the people who don't care about folks like us, who put us down, tell us we're sick, and don't show us any respect."

He didn't notice the odd way that Ida looked his way, with tilted head, and then stared at him.

They pulled into the yard and parked beside Larry's still empty spot.

Ida got out of the car with purpose and said flatly, "I'm going to take a walk and call Sally." She marched off.

"Don't mention anything about the bank," Louis called.

"I'm not stupid Louie," she yelled back.

In the forty minutes before Ida returned, Louis had nurtured his anxiety that she would say something to Sally about the bank robbery. Otherwise, he spent the time cleaning fish and making dinner.

Something was obviously different about Ida when she got back. Her demeanour was sanguine. Louis wasn't perceptive enough to imagine any reason for this other than that time away had allowed her a chance to calm down. But the truth was that something more significant had occurred.

What Louis had picked up on, without realizing it, was Ida's self-affirmation; her refusal to accept the sort of treatment that she'd too often accepted in the past. She had come to realize that, for once, she was angry at Louis in a way that would never dissipate. Things were over. Not that she was going to say so right now. At least her anger would help her, finally, to reclaim some dignity.

Ida sat down in the kitchen and dispassionately looked about while Louis put two plates of fried trout and Larry's tinned beans on the table. She would pretend to like the fish in spite of fact that the thought of eating something that wasn't distanced from its living form by having been purchased in a store, was disgusting.

Her gaze played over a ten-year-old calendar on the wall. It fit with the old furniture, giving the place a time capsule feel. She wondered if Larry was trying to freeze time.

And she pondered the old-fashioned, repulsive, mossy

green colour of the painted wooden board on the walls and cupboards: hospital or school chic. No more dumps like this and no more stolen tins of food, she thought. She was going to demand something more from now on.

"So'd Sally get the job?" Louis asked, more to confirm from the tone of her response whether Ida had indeed calmed down than from any particular interest in Sally. He was pleased that Ida didn't appear to be brooding the way she sometimes did, so no need to navigate around anger. She seemed a little aloof, some coolness in her eyes, but he had only ever found unavailability arousing. He smiled in her general direction.

"She doesn't know. Apparently the hiring was put on hold. Sally thinks they probably cancelled the job but Billy-boy doesn't want to say so cus he's got the hots for her and wants to stay in touch. She's feeling pretty pissed off at men – she tends to generalize – and with looking for work." Ida cut herself off, not wanting to be saying anything more.

They ate in silence after that and avoided talking about bank robbery.

"What's with all these pictures of Indian mystics?" Ida asked, waving her hand in the direction of several framed photos on the walls of Indian holy men.

"Don't know," Louis said thoughtfully. "Hare Krishna or something, I guess. I really don't know my brother at all."

16.

the guy was not to be trusted

Detective Swain placidly watched Detective Rose as he typed one-handed with intense concentration. Rose was researching 'Mac's Trucking' on the internet, which was stupid because Swain had already told him what he was going to find: that it was a small outfit way the fuck out in Winnipeg. It was clear they were going to have to reach out to the Winnipeg police force to get some information on Cutter, since that's where he was probably from.

He's a big fucker, Swain thought as he watched Rose, fascinated with how the man's beefy legs and arms stretched his clothing to the limit: a regular L'il Abner. He watched Rose scrunch his face up close to the computer monitor and wondered why the guy didn't just get some glasses. You'd think someone who spent hours and hours working on his muscles, and thinking about his looks, would spend a bit of time looking after something practical.

The two men were sitting in Rose's office, across the hall from Swain's, who was here to discuss the Stone Cutter murder that was being handled by Rose.

It had become apparent that the two detectives were working opposite ends of the same case when Swain called Rose to ask about the late owner of a baseball cap found on the farm of a drug kingpin and murderer. He informed his colleague that impossibly, since the cap had been wet when found, that testing had discovered some fingerprints on the inside of it; on the stiff area at the bottom that is always pressed against the wearer's head.

One print belonged to the late Stonewall Cutter, confirming that this was the cap that had gone missing from the murder scene. Three other prints belonged to an unknown person and matched several that were found in the apartment of the deceased victim. And a single print belonged to one Lemony Boissoneault. Swain's team had already gone to the media in their search for him and they were now hoping for some further help from Rose.

From boredom, while Rose typed and squinted, Swain strained to hear the voices coming from a nearby office.

He stood and looked out the window at the upscale townhouses across the street. Swain had once lived there when the buildings consisted of rundown flats.

"I'm getting the same thing as you about Cutter," Rose said, still squinting at the computer monitor. "What do you make of the fact that the hat was at the farm? Think the kid was there?"

"Maybe," answered Swain. "Lemony's a biker, with the Triceps, so he probably made contact with the hat at the farm. He hangs out there."

"And, we know he wasn't at Cutter's apartment, or at least didn't leave any prints there. So It's likely that whoever was at Cutter's, and left prints all over, is a biker as well."

"It would explain how the hat made its way to the farm."

"Right. We know that Cutter was a small-time dealer so it's likely the farm is where he got his supply," said Rose. "We're convinced that he was thrown from his balcony – there was definitely a fight there – meaning we'd very much like to know who this biker is that gave Boissoneault his cap. Or do you think that he just found it?"

"No I don't, but it's the kind of thing his lawyer will say and you can't refute it."

"So let's brainstorm some theories about the mystery man who walked off with Cutter's cap. He has no prints on record anywhere. He's either very young or very careful. I mean assuming he's not just some law-abiding upstanding citizen."

Swain snorted in response.

"So the mystery man's our suspect. Is he a hitman?" Rose asked.

"Maybe. He could have given Lemony the hat as a sign he completed the job. And Lemony was likely working for Hayes."

"But does a hit make sense?"

"It strikes me as unlikely if you mean that Hayes brought in an outside hitman for some kid who ripped him off for a few grand or something."

"I agree," Rose nodded. "But we can't rule it out."

A pause ensued while both men thought.

"So, you're gonna follow up with Winnipeg to see what you can get on the kid," said Swain, "and I'll talk to Hayes to try and track down Lemony."

"I'm thinkin' that the guy who's going to tell us what we want to know is Lemony."

Swain, who was still standing, pointed over Rose's shoulder, towards the window, and the road that was visible beyond. "You know I used to live across the street, 'bout halfway down the block."

"Ah," said Rose, as if this was news. Someone had mentioned it when Swain's name came up that morning. Rose knew the exact house and wondered if Swain was implying he'd lived in the upscale places that sat there now instead of the dumps that had been there up until a few years ago. How much do you trust a guy who would do that?

17.

Thursday: even the stock market has some risk

At breakfast, with a slightly contemptuous look on her face, as if they were all evident charlatans, Ida again scanned the photos of the Indian holy men on Larry's kitchen wall and wondered how he had come to an awareness of these guys when he lived out here in a remote cottage. She would have thought that, given his interests, that the kitchen would have been full of brown rice and vegetables rather than wieners and the same sort of crap that Louis ate.

She continued to look at the photos long after her interest waned rather than watch Louis eat. The food rolled around in his open maw, snapping with every chew. He was beginning to disgust her. She knew he had a deviated septum so needed to breathe through his mouth while he was chewing, but she was no longer inclined to be generous.

Louis clandestinely eyed Ida. She wasn't touching her eggs but he didn't want to ask why, afraid of what she might say. Like the cartoon Road Runner, you can delay plummeting off the cliff only so long as you don't acknowledge that you've stepped over the edge. You won't get the response you don't want as long as you don't ask the question. As he ate though, Louis was working himself up to say something. He had to; time was running out.

"I need to know now what you decided about the bank," he said with studied casualness, as if by his tone he could minimize the extreme nature of the request. "If we're gonna do it we should be gettin' ourselves a car and the stuff we'll need."

Ida laughed softly then coyly looked into Louis's eyes – for a long time. Her lightness drifted across the table till Louis smiled back, as if sharing an intimacy, but it was actually only a complete lack of sincerity that connected them.

"I don't know what makes you think I was deciding about the bank," Ida said. "I never said I was. You always assume..." She continued to stare at Louis. "I have no interest in going to jail," she added in a serious tone.

"Yeah, yeah, that's understandable. Maybe I came at you too abruptly, or didn't explain it well enough, how little risk there is; but we can do this. They won't be expectin' it and we can get back here in about twenty minutes. No one's gonna think that a local was involved. They'll be stoppin' cars on the highway. We'll stay here and leave a few days later."

"So, you're telling me there's nothing to worry about?"

Louis looked out the window to a cloudless sky, the sun shining like it was trying to redeem itself after an earlier rain. "Naw, that'd be bullshit, there's always some risk. Even the stock market has some risk; more than this though."

"If the cops came snooping around afterwards, they'll see the stolen car."

"We can move the shit out from in front of the garage door, put the car inside and then put the stuff back. Any cop coming by won't suspect a thing. They won't even know anyone's here."

"I don't know." More coyness. A trace of a smile.

"Sometimes you gotta take a risk in life."

"Okay," Ida said abruptly with decisiveness, slapping the table.

"Okay?" Louis looked at her for some help.

"Okay, I'll do it."

Ida's beatific smile brought on a split second of elation from Louis followed by a sudden sense of remorse. He felt guilty thinking he'd manipulated her, poor thing, twisting her around his little finger. He'd been contemplating this robbery for the past year and had adjusted himself to the idea of potentially getting caught by rationalizing that a jail term would be a fitting punishment for his past deeds, so somehow earned. It struck him now that, for Ida, it would be a disaster.

Blinded by a belief in his powers of persuasion, Louis could not discern that Ida's conversion was ludicrous, that it had been too easy to talk her into helping him. He was naïve enough to believe that in less than twenty-four hours someone who hated him and was repulsed by the idea of committing a crime could be convinced to help him rob a bank.

And, had he been less convinced of his own Svengali-like powers, and that Ida was easily manipulatable, he would have seen in her coyness that she had already made her mind up to involve herself with the robbery when she sat down for breakfast and had been merely feigning reluctance. Any reasonable person would have been suspicious about why she had changed her mind about the robbery with so little effort.

Ida, meanwhile, didn't know whether to be offended or pleased. Sadly, she had been correct. Louis believed that she was so simple that he could talk her into robbing a bank. He couldn't imagine that she might be manipulating him. She was invisible to him. He never saw the person behind the facade because he never looked.

Ida drove them eighty kilometres north to a small city of 15,000. She followed Louis's directions.

On the trip, they followed a circuitous route along back roads to avoid the possibility of a cop spotting the Capri. The highways, in this part of the world, were blasted through granite, creating passages between high walls of jagged rock marked by swirling greys, black, coral and a startlingly bright white. But the back roads went over the hills, following the contours of the land, through stands of giant poplar, birch, jack pine, cedar, hemlock and sugar maple. They wound past farms originally settled with a view to their proximity to one of the small towns scattered along the rail lines.

Ida's eyes went continuously to the rear-view mirror, as if expecting a cop to emerge at any moment. "So you spent some time around here?" she said to Louis, trying to distract herself from the stress of cruising in a stolen purple car.

"Some," said Louis. "We used to come up here fishin' and for a year lived about twenty klicks away. This school we're gonna pass in a minute has a baseball diamond behind it. I used to play there sometimes with my school team. You'd get eaten in the outfield from bugs cus it backs onto the bush."

"I played baseball for awhile," said Ida flatly.

Louis looked sceptical.

"Yeah, Yeah," said Ida. "I know. You're thinking I must have been pretty crappy but I wasn't. Baseball didn't turn out

84

great though. It's why I quit school…to avoid further embarrassment."

"Explain."

"We were playing at another high school in the championship game. I was the catcher. It was two to one and we were about to win. The other team was up to bat in the bottom of the ninth. Two outs. Player on second… You with me?"

"Yeah, I get it. Guy on second and two out. Your team's leading by a run."

"Right. So our pitcher throws a pitch and their batter smacks the ball to left field. Our fielder picks it up and fires it back to the shortstop who throws it on to me at home plate. I see the girl on second, out of the corner of my eye, making for third. I'm on top of things. I see the batter go round first but I don't throw to second because I know the runner who's on third will stay there because I have the ball, and as long as the run doesn't score we're good."

"Okay."

"And that's when my school career came to an end. All of a sudden my teammates started pointing and yelling, 'Back! Back!' The whole friggin' bench was jumping up and down and screaming their lungs out. So I panicked. What they were pointing to was that the runner had rounded third, hoping to score if I threw to second, and that she had come so far past the base that if I threw the ball to third we'd catch her in a run down. She was frozen halfway between the bases. The problem was, I didn't understand. I didn't have a fucking clue what they were yelling about but they kept screaming. All I picked up on was the urgency. These girls and our coach were yelling, 'Back! Back!' so figuring I had to do something but not knowing what it was, I acted, and you'll never guess what I did."

"Nothing?"

"I wish. That would have been okay but, no, I wound up and threw the ball back to the left fielder who'd thrown the ball to me. She was running to back up the third baseman during a rundown."

"Naw. You're kidding me."

"Nope. And not only did the girl on third run home but the one who got the hit scored too. She had never stopped running and I ended up throwing the ball way over the head of the left fielder. Adrenalin, I guess. So, game over. We lose three to two."

"Shit."

"I was completely humiliated and back at school people just went on and on about it. Called me 'retard' after that. It was near the end of grade eleven. It was only a few weeks to go but I never went back – had damn good marks too – but I didn't want to see anyone I went to school with ever again."

"That sounds pretty extreme."

"It was, but that's the way I felt. Even now I'm forcing myself to laugh about it when I tell you, but it was horrid. No one shut up about it. I felt like an idiot. You want to kill yourself. So I went to live with my father in the city."

The conversation fell off after that and the two drove in silence.

Ida dropped Louis off in a shopping mall parking lot. They had driven for an hour and a half. She turned the car around and headed for home following the detailed directions written on the paper that Louis had prepared for her.

Louis walked towards the mall with a tremendous sense of relief to be out of Ida's presence. He'd begun to absorb the tension she was exuding. Suddenly his step was sprightly. Things were beginning to work out. The money from the robbery would be the seed money to facilitate his ambition to buy a little camper and follow the horses to meets around North America. Confident he could make a bit of income from gambling, he would stay cheap at campgrounds instead of boondocking it one night at a time in Target and Walmart parking lots. He wanted to be free of all encumbrances, obligations and memories from his life to date. It was the desire to be a nomad, a lifestyle of autonomy versus the life of a refugee that he had now. A refutation of the idea that homelessness was a sign of failure and sickness, and that it should be stamped out because the homeless were either viewed as repulsive or in need of kindness.

Louis went through the mall and shoplifted two pairs of gloves, a suit of men's clothes for Ida, and some pantyhose to cover their faces during the robbery. The clothes were oversized: big enough for Louis to wear out of the store over his street clothes and big enough that Ida could stuff them with rags to change her shape. As long as she kept her mouth shut, and let him do all the talking, she would create the illusion of being a man.

Louis left the mall and began to walk up and down the rows of cars hoping to find one with an unlocked door so he wouldn't need to smash a window. That would probably set off an alarm and, if it didn't, it would still draw attention.

On his third aisle, Louis came across an old, unlocked silver Civic. Unlike the purple Capri, stolen because it was flashy, he now wanted something common, and a silver Civic, by his reckoning, was about as common as it got. Louis climbed inside, bent down, stripped the starter, battery, and ignition wires, twisted the latter two together and then touched the starter wire to the join. The car's engine came to life. Now came the hard part. He preferred to grab cars with Joseph because it was much easier to break the lock pin with two people, but he was on his own today. Back and forth he wrenched the steering wheel until he eventually heard the blessed click that released the wheel and the transmission.

On the way home Louis drove by the bank that would be their target the next morning. It sat on the main drag in a village of five hundred or so souls and it was only a few blocks in every direction to open country.

Driving away from the bank, in the direction of his brother's place, he looked for a spot where he could stash the car in the morning. It had to be secluded enough that no one would spot the Civic before the robbery, as it sat waiting. Or the abandoned Capri immediately after they did the post-robbery exchange.

Cruising slowly along the highway, keeping an eye out for other traffic, Louis soon spied the perfect location: an overgrown farmer's access trail that started at the highway, ran down through the ditch, and then along the edge of a hay field. There was a thick stand of trees between the road and the start of the field. It would be as easy as pie to follow the trail from the highway and, at the field, to swing left and drive into the corn. The car could be parked there, behind the trees, and out of sight from passing traffic. The spot couldn't be more than a kilometre outside of the town so it was the perfect location in every respect.

With that settled, he drove home and parked the Civic in his brother's empty spot where it would stay overnight.

For the rest of the day, back at Larry's, Ida and Louis went over the plan.

They tried on their masks, and Ida put on the men's clothing; including the stuffing. Louis sized her up and pronounced that she'd pass as a man.

He marked out the layout of the bank's interior on the ground in front of the house, using stones. It was nowhere close to the actual dimensions, but it gave a reasonable approximation of the set up.

Together, the aspiring robbers walked through the steps they would take during the robbery, with Louis choreographing and calling out instructions. He rehearsed his lines and twice counselled Ida to keep silent in order to get used to the idea.

Ida obeyed in earnest, nodding her head.

The basics of the scheme were that Louis would position himself behind the bank's counter at a moment when the place was empty of customers, and after Ida had locked the front door. Louis would cover all employees with the handgun, and do all the talking, while Ida retrieved the money. They would then leave. The whole thing was expected to take about forty seconds. The Capri would be sitting at the curb and hopefully someone would spot it so that word would go out to be on the lookout for a purple car. Louis and Ida would start out driving north on the main drag (the opposite direction to their ultimate destination) but once out of sight of the bank they would tail back along a side street. At the sound end of town they'd return to the main drag, turn south, and head for the Civic hidden in the cornfield where they'd switch cars. What could go wrong?

Louis patiently answered Ida's many questions about exactly where they would make the car transfer and how long it would take to get there. He assured her again how he was confident the plan was foolproof.

"We ain't gettin' caught baby," he said with bravado, then dropping his voice added, "but there's always that one in a million chance, so just remember that if we ever do get picked up you should say I held the handgun on you once we got to Larry's, and I forced you to go along cus I needed a second person. That I told you if you co-operated I'd let you out of the car in the first town we came to after the robbery. And if you didn't, I'd kill you. If we both tell exactly the same story then the cops'll buy it."

Later at dinner, eating fish again, Louis went into even more precise detail about their story if caught; the when, where and how. "It'll make it more convincing the more detailed it is; if that one in a million chance we need it actually happens."

They were ready. That evening Louis rearranged the stuff in the garage to make room for the Civic. He also moved some old tires that were stacked in front of the garage door, and completely wiped down the Capri. Tomorrow they would wear gloves when they took turns driving it.

18.

Friday. Socrates is a person?

It was going on for one AM. Reg was yawning as he spoke. "I wouldn't mind bein' a cop like the old man, you know? After I got the training I mean. He said he'd help me. But like, when's he ever done that before. It's the reason I've got so many problems. It's not equipping a kid right for the world, you know?"

No answer.

"Eh?"

No answer.

"You know what I mean?"

"Yes," Lawrence finally replied.

"What I'd like to be is a musician. Play country. I wish he'd support me doin' that." Reg began singing low.

"It doesn't matter whether your father has anything to do with you or not. It's irrelevant to how well you turn out. Socrates said that."

Reg stopped singing. "Socrates is a person?"

"A Greek philosopher."

"Ah." It was just as Reg had suspected apparently.

Discussions with Reg always involved a lot of explaining but Lawrence didn't mind. "I have to relieve myself. Excuse me," he said suddenly, popping up and starting down towards the river.

Reg hated this. His sleepiness went into remission the instant Lawrence disappeared from sight. Reg sat up and peered at the bush, all senses on alert because of his unholy and irrational fear of bears. His terror went back to a night spent alone in a cabin when he was a kid. A bear began scratching around and in his youthful paranoia Reg had imagined it might tear down the door.

He reached for the hatchet and held it in his lap, ready for use. The hatchet always accompanied him when camping; otherwise it stayed in the shed behind the house. Thousands of times, growing up, he'd thrown it at trees. Reg, Indian brave on the warpath. And he was damn accurate with it.

90

It won't be long, he comforted himself, till he and Lawrence would leave. This was to be their last night on this trip, he'd decided, and had just broken the news to his friend. "Enough," he'd said, "I don't mind one night camping here and there, I know you like it, but I'm not going to stay out here till your brother leaves. I want to go back." Lawrence wasn't happy, being forced to go home – even Reg could tell – but it was too bloody bad. Getting some cash from selling smokes was nice but this camping shit was for the birds.

Lawrence went down to the creek, urinated, walked out on some rocks that protruded above the surface and hopscotched downstream, going rock to rock in the moonlight. He was disturbed by Reg's insistence on going home. It was a surprising bit of assertiveness, but Lawrence knew there was no point questioning it, with Reg being so adamant. And it didn't matter, he rationalized, since he'd all but decided to have another go at suicide and hopefully get better results than he'd gotten last time. All that was left was to set the date. It would have been nice to enjoy his last few days however.

Lawrence jumped back to the riverbank when he saw an opening through the dark curtain of branches overhanging the water.

He immediately turned around and stood there, watching the stream.

Foam congregated behind boulders in the moving water, and glistened. The night was clear and the sky blasted with stars. This was so much nicer than watching TV at home with two strangers. It was peaceful, which Lawrence often thought was odd in a way. Lethe, the spirit of the river, brought forgetfulness and peace, but she was a daughter of Eris, the goddess of strife, so sister of the Phonoi, the spirits who oversee murder, killing and slaughter. Out of strife flowed violence and death. Lawrence had told himself, that in the end, maybe all the offspring of Eris were alike in that they eventually brought peace – even through murder.

Lawrence climbed the bank. He had travelled about fifteen metres downriver, and gone past the campsite, so at the top of the bank he turned and trudged his way back through the bush towards the dwindling remains of the campfire.

Reg heard. Something was crunching through the bush behind him, coming his way!

He turned, gripping the hatchet as he awaited the impending bear attack. The shadowy figure he saw was crashing through the bush. Headed his way. It was almost his height. A monster of a black bear!

In desperation, Reg looked back over his shoulder. Why the fuck didn't Lawrence hurry up? Reg raised his hatchet. All those years of throwing it against the trees round back of the barn were about to pay off.

When the last of the bushes at the edge of the clearing shook with the bear's presence, Reg flung the hatchet with all his might and heard the soft gush of it sinking into its target.

19.

summoned by her ladyship

Ida's friend Sally arose in the middle of the night. She turned on a small bedside lamp and got dressed in clothes that she'd laid out earlier. Best to have a plan then turn off your brain. That way you didn't chicken out. The final touches were red lipstick and hair swept to the side, like the way it was worn by the stars of those movies from the forties that she loved: like Lauren Bacall in *The Big Sleep*, like Gene Tierney in *Laura*.

Her room was tiny, with faux Victorian trimmings. Two of the walls were crammed with mounted plates. Not three walls. Not four walls. Two. More would be excessive, she felt, even though she kept collecting plates and had nearly exhausted every inch of space. Ida said she'd taken plate collecting to the extreme, making it a 'dishopline', a word of her own invention. No one ever understood the joke.

Sally crept slowly and gingerly down the stairs. It wouldn't do to wake anyone. Only two days ago she'd been summoned by her ladyship to that one's first floor room, led there by the dumb one, to wait anxiously and bite her nails, and be told, finally, that she must find alternate accommodations because there were four others living in the house and she was at war with three of them. For months Sally had been trying unsuccessfully to reconcile with the group but it had turned out to be a waste of time.

Ten minutes later she turned onto the highway, and headed north. She lowered the visor and glanced at herself in the mirror on the back of it. She was undoubtedly beautiful, she told herself. She could have, should have, made it as a model or actress. Those had always been her goals from the time she was small, a natural who loved the spotlight, but she had met up with a child molester at age ten.

The perpetrator was Anthony Chadwick, acclaimed as one of the country's premier playwrights and father of Milo, Sally's best friend and neighbour. It was Anthony who had turned Milo on to acting and he who'd introduced it to Sally.

Sally said nothing to anyone about the incident, and life went on. But its effects never left her.

The incident had almost passed into the dark corners of her memory, especially after Anthony Chadwick died from cancer when Sally was a sophomore in high school, and it would have been nice if it had settled in there, but it didn't.

In their final year of high school, Milo and Sally both decided to pursue theatre training after graduation, and to further their ambitions they hoped to land the lead roles in the school's big spring production.

But the teacher selected a play called *Little Small*, a three-act drama whose main character was based on Anthony Chadwick. The play's selection was meant as a tribute.

Sally and Milo auditioned, and won the parts they wanted.

There would be press interviews, they were told, good for their careers, and to expect a love-in for Chadwick. The undoubted angle the press would pounce on, it was speculated, was that his son was starring in the play.

At first, Sally thought, what the hell, it doesn't matter, but as time went on she felt that she couldn't glorify anyone who would molest a child, regardless of how the victim had handled it, so she quit the production.

But what to say to Milo? He didn't understand why she'd quit. He felt hurt. This was to be a tribute to his father after all. Sally debated with herself about whether to tell him the real reason why she'd dropped out, but decided, in the end, that she couldn't. Had she done so, the only person that would be hurt by the revelation would be Milo, and he'd done nothing wrong.

So instead, she told him she'd dropped out because she'd lost interest in theatre, and as further proof, to appear genuine, she didn't pursue her education in theatre – or anything else – at college in the fall.

So she ended up being a victim after all, ironically, in part, so as not to make herself into a victim and forever be defined as such. She had sacrificed much for love of her victimizer's son and his illusions; a boy who wasn't even her lover.

At age nineteen, Sally went to work at The Plastic Man and met Ida. Sally hated it there but stayed. She used to

94

complain that it was like being trapped in a desert-like environment of people scrabbling to get by, 'working for water'.

"We're all paying for things we didn't do," she often told Ida.

20.

an endless bibliography in search of a text

Lemony stared into the dark. He was laying on his back, waiting for morning, and thinking about how, in a few hours, he'd be back in the city. He was anxious to be home because of the impending launch of his first book, an 800 page rambling tome to be published by No Holds Bard Books that one advance reviewer had described as *'an endless bibliography in search of a text'*. Another wrote that, *'Its beginning, middle and end occur simultaneously in a non-linear tour de force'*, which was another way of saying that the book went nowhere and was about nothing.

Lemony had already been asked to write a new book, a self-helper about how to find a literary agent; an offer he had modestly declined at first and only consented to in the end because of relentless pursuit. He envisioned writing it in the unlikely manner of a prose poem and had sketched out chapters in the dark of early morning with titles like, *'Phone or letter?'*, *'The old bait and switch'*, and *'Using the distraction tactic'*. His publisher was concerned because the chapter titles sounded like nonsense.

It had been another miserable night spent in the barn's loft, sweating like he had a fever and struggling to breathe the heavy air. If it had been earlier he would have slipped down the ladders, as he often did, down to the underground bunker to stretch out on a blanket beside the metal table. Every night he'd climb to the loft, sick of the bunker, but eventually, in the middle of most nights, the unbearable air drove him back downstairs.

A short time later, Lemony got up, along with the rest of the guys and, on his first foray of the day, walked under the blessing of a burnt orange sunlight that saturated the landscape. A glorious morning had finally come. For most of the past ten days, on his trips to and from the farmhouse, Lemony had dodged the rain that bullied him, as if he'd offended some vengeful god.

The men took their places around big tables in the kitchen

and dining room. Most just had coffee because they couldn't be bothered to cook anything for themselves. Some talked and the others listened to the radio playing too loud to be just wallpaper. So it was that four people, including Lemony, heard when the announcer mentioned that Lawrence (Lemony) Boissoneault was wanted as a person of interest in the suspicious death of a young city man.

Those who'd heard fell silent and the others, aware from this reaction that something of significance had been said, stopped talking and looked around in confusion, until eventually following the gaze of those staring in Lemony's direction.

"Hey man, that's you," Fish needlessly advised him.

Voices chimed up with questions about the announcement, which Lemony answered simply with a shrug and a look of incomprehension.

"What? What's that?" demanded Jaycee. Speaking, as always, in a manner that staked a claim to being queen of the house.

"There was this news report on the radio that said Lemony is a suspect in a murder," someone answered.

"No," another corrected, "a person of interest."

"He has no idea what it's about," a third voice explained.

"Jack is gonna be furious," accused Jaycee. "You better get outta here Lemony before the cops come round. Jack won't like that and he won't want you here when he gets back tomorrow or the next day."

Jaycee had no authority – everyone knew that – and they knew she had no real influence on Jack. When Jack was with the boys down in the bunker it was clear from his crude comments that he saw Jaycee as a conquest only. He'd even once offered her to Lemony for a night saying she owed it to him as a thank you for some work on the computer Lemony had done for her.

"What you wanna do," someone told Lemony, ignoring Jaycee, "is to stay here and plan your course of action. Get down the hole if the cops come around. Maybe wait for a few days till things settle down. Jack'll understand."

Jaycee looked furious.

Lemony wasn't at all sure that Jack would understand. He was confused by Jack, and like everyone else there, afraid of him. Jack was a slippery bastard, a killer, and the atmosphere he'd created on the farm was poison. People were encouraged to squeal on each other, presumably to undermine possible alliances, so everyone kept personal stuff to themselves and horse-traded with their cronies to keep past secrets from being relayed to Jack.

Lemony's view was that Jack had no loyalty to him, nor did the guy see him as a friend, in spite of the offer of Jaycee for a night. That was just grandstanding to show his power. It didn't take Lemony long to decide that Jack would be pissed if he stayed around. His boss was as paranoid as they come.

In spite of this, Lemony figured his best option was to stick around the farm for a few days, at least until Jack got back and kicked him out. It would give him a chance to figure out what to do.

As everyone filtered out of the kitchen, and the first bait and switch vehicle headed to town, Lemony wondered why the police would be after him. The working hypothesis he developed was that one of his friends had killed someone, that the cops were aware of his connection to the killer, and that they wanted to dig for information. Things would blow over in time, especially if the cops found the culprit.

Jaycee stalked around the kitchen, scowling and slamming cupboards.

"You going?" she demanded of Lemony when there was just the two of them left in the house.

"I'm heading down to the barn," he answered calmly, standing up, and walking out the door.

As he went past the growling German Shepherd and fended off the bounding collie nudging his side, his thoughts were on Jack's money stash. One night when Lemony had been sleeping in the bunker he'd awoken to see Jack, flashlight in hand, unscrewing the metal plate on the floor. His next actions made it obvious that he was opening a hidden safe and putting something in it. Jack obviously didn't know anyone was there. Lemony could only imagine the contents of the safe. It was likely loaded with drug money

98

that Jack didn't want to keep in the house or put in the bank.

After Jack had left, Lemony managed to remove the plate and scrutinized the safe. It was small and laid into the cement, but didn't appear to be attached. Thinking about it subsequently, he always wondered if maybe it could be pried loose from the recess and removed from the property to be opened later, at leisure.

Lemony hadn't thought about the safe for awhile. To touch it could be suicide, he knew. But he thought about it now. It looked like it was time to split, and he'd need some big money if he was going to lay low for awhile. Not to mention that it would be satisfying to pay Jack back for the way he'd been treated.

21.

this purple monster will be all over the news

The criminal duo talked while standing beside the stolen cars that were idling outside Larry's front door. Both wore gloves and Ida wore her man outfit, appropriately stuffed. In spite of that, Louis thought of Bonnie and Clyde and felt the erotic charge that comes from the mixing of sex and crime.

"It'll take us thirty minutes to get to where we stash the cars," Louis said.

Once again they were going to take a circuitous route so that afterwards, if someone came forward to say they'd seen the purple Capri approaching the hiding spot, they would tell of it coming from the north instead of the direction of Larry's.

"Give me a five minute head start so you're not sittin' at the side of the road while I stash the Civic," Louis said. "Drive at the speed limit, and no faster, and if it happens you catch up to me, as soon as you see me in the distance, slow down, no, find somewhere to stop for a couple of minutes. I want you to time the pick up so that all you do is stop on the shoulder for a second while I jump into the Capri. You understand?"

"Yes." Ida stared at the ground while doing her best to regulate her breathing. She looked like a player on the sidelines of a football game getting a pep talk from the coach before being sent in. She hated all sports.

"And slow down or speed up if there's another car close to you. I don't want anyone to see me when you pick me up cus I won't have my mask on."

Ida's head, with its mound of hair the colour of an old penny, now tied in a knot, went up and down in agreement.

Louis looked concerned. "Don't worry, we'll be back here in no time. We're just gonna whip into the bank, dump the Capri, and come straight back here. Then we'll have some lunch." 'A normal day out' his tone seemed to say; no worry, just routine.

"Make sure you follow the plan Louie!" Ida said, raising her head to make eye contact. "No sudden changes. The only reason I let you talk me into this is because we have a fixed plan."

"Yeah, of course. And everything's gonna go according to it. Trust me."

Ida exhaled deeply and slowly.

A short time later, Louis drove the Civic onto the shoulder, down a very slight embankment, and along a farmer's trail to the edge of a cornfield. He stopped, did a three point turn, taking out some cornstalks, and backed the car along the edge of the field so it was out of sight of the road.

He walked back to the highway and stood behind a large tree near the shoulder. When he saw the purple Capri rounding a bend a half kilometre away, and after a quick check told him nothing was coming in the opposite direction, he moved to the edge of the road and waived down Ida.

Louis took over the driving. Arriving in the town of Carmel, minutes later, he guided the Capri to a spot in front of a two-storey brick building on the main drag with the words '*Public Library 1923*' embossed on a strip of concrete above the front doors. Above that was a blue wooden sign reading, '*Carmel Farmer's Co-operative Credit Union*'.

It was a curbless main drag with no sidewalks; just a paved shoulder along the edge of the highway where it passed through the town. A typical country village.

Neither robber moved.

Louis scanned the road ahead.

Ida regulated her breathing like she was in a Lamaze class. Ducking her head down to look up at the building, she said accusingly, "It's a credit union."

"So? Credit union, bank, same thing."

As Louis climbed out of the car he squeezed his nose between the thumb and forefinger of his right hand, in a way that obscured most of his face. He then began rubbing his nose, as if it was sore, with the flat of his hand.

Immediately on entering the credit union, he turned his back toward the tellers while pretending to look out the window, craning his neck as if watching for someone. A quick look had told him there was only one customer.

Outside, Ida gripped her pantyhose mask and watched.

101

The door of the credit union opened and an old lady exited.

Louis surreptitiously beckoned Ida forward. He remained standing at the window after that, still facing the street, apparently waiting for someone. The teller, who'd drawn that conclusion about what he was doing, returned to her work.

With a final look around, Ida pulled the pantyhose over her head and climbed out of the car. This was the cue for Louis to don his own mask and bring out his handgun.

The sole teller looked up as Ida came through the door and then locked it.

By that time, Louis was running toward the counter, then stepping behind it.

The teller turned to see his handgun pointed at her.

A second teller emerged from the hallway to the offices. She froze when she saw Louis's gun. Her mouth fell open and she mewed despairingly.

"Open your cash drawers then back up to the wall and raise your hands," Louis said.

The tellers obeyed, and were soon inching backwards, arms in the air.

"You too," Louis added, waving his gun in the direction of an older woman sitting at a desk to his left. Until then she'd been observing, as if she was watching TV, but suddenly snapped to life realizing that she too was involved in what was happening. She moved to stand beside her colleagues, with arms extended over her head.

Ida had been half disbelieving of Louis's description of the bank as out of step with the times but the worn hardwood floors, wooden counter and lack of a guard, all spoke of an independent old-fashioned institution. In response to a nod from her partner, she ran around behind the counter to retrieve money from the teller's drawers, checking for dye packs as she went.

Louis watched over the three employees, one standing immobile and two attempting to do the same but obviously shaking. Some distant laughing startled him. With a surge of fear of his own he looked about. He'd forgotten about the offices. Stupid, he thought. Stupid, stupid! Why hadn't Ida asked about offices? An obvious question... Leave it. People in closed offices. Nothing to worry about. Why involve them needlessly?

Exhilaration swept in as the anxiety leaked out. Luck was on his side, he thought. And the feeling may have been justified. Just to find a bank or credit union in farm country that wasn't jammed with customers was akin to a miracle; something that said the gods of robbery were looking kindly down on him.

Ida came out from behind the counter and raised the plastic bag in her hand for Louis to see she was done.

"Now," he said to the three women behind the counter, "sit down on the floor." He spoke in a whispered tone.

The women sat.

"Stay there." He continued to hold his gun on them while glancing at Ida over his shoulder. She had gone to the window to check for street traffic. Louis heard the click of the door unlocking. The getting was good, it said. Within seconds they were gone.

Back in the Capri, masks still on, Louis handed the handgun to Ida and drove. Straight ahead, going north. Right at the first street, right again. Back through town. Another right, then a left, and they were now heading south.

As soon as they were clear of the town limit, and up to speed, they removed their masks.

Soon after, Louis decelerated, swung the car onto the shoulder and made a hard turn to bounce down the same farmer's trail he'd been over earlier. On reaching the Civic, he swung the Capri into the cornfield.

Not a word had been uttered until now. "Keep your gloves on 'til you're out of the car," Louis said.

They climbed out of the Capri with Ida still holding the gun. The now useless keys were left in the ignition.

Louis popped the trunk of the Civic, pulled off his gloves and unbuttoned his shirt. These were thrown into the trunk along with his pantyhose mask. Like Ida, he had a full set of clothes on under his robbery outfit.

"You got the gun?" he asked over his shoulder as he undid his pants and slid them down.

"Yeah Louie, I got it."

He pulled his pants over his shoes, and looked up at Ida as he tossed them into the trunk of the Civic. She was standing still.

"Don't freeze up now. You gotta get your costume off. We gotta move it!" Louis said.

Shaken back to life, Ida quickly began removing her outfit.

When Louis was down to his getaway clothes he hot wired the Civic. Climbing out of the driver's seat he came face to face with Ida. She held the handgun in both hands the way she'd seen it done in the movies. It was pointed in the direction of Louis's head.

"Don't do that," he said casually, smiling. "You finished?"

It had been too big a cognitive jump for Louis to immediately take in what was happening but he suddenly cottoned on to the idea that this was serious. He stopped, immobilized. "What are you…"

"Put your hands on top of your head Louis," said a second woman's voice, coming from behind him.

He hesitated, recognizing the voice, and slowly lifted his arms in response to the feel of a large knife pressed to the back of his neck.

Sally stepped around him, the knife sliding along Louis's skin. She took two brisk steps backward and took the handgun from Ida.

"What the fuck Sally?" Louis said.

"Just keep your hands up," she answered. "Don't get heroic. The last thing I want to do is shoot you, but I will. You know I will."

Louis kept his arms raised while Sally went past him. She opened the passenger door of the Capri and snatched up the keys.

"Ida!" Louis implored, looking pleadingly in her direction. "Don't do this."

Ida said nothing. She caught the keys lobbed to her by Sally.

Louis saw the trunk of the Capri swing upward.

"Now climb in," said Sally. She made her way, to behind Louis, and nudged his back with the barrel of the gun.

"In the Capri?"

"Yeah."

"Jeez. C'mon Sally. I'll suffocate."

"That's bullshit and you know it."

Louis inched his way toward the purple car and straddled one leg over the edge of the trunk. Turning to eye Sally he lowered himself down and, unable to manage the climb with his hands above his head, fell the last bit of the way. He grunted.

"Listen Louie," said Ida, looking down at Louis, laying on his back, arms still partially raised. "I know you can get out of the car, I mean, after all the cars you've stolen over the years. I'm not trying to set you up to get caught, but if you do, I trust you won't give the cops my name. Remember, you've told me about a dozen crimes you've committed; especially yesterday when you were trying to convince me that you're an experienced criminal and I shouldn't be worried about getting caught. I'll tell the cops about every one of them. At least one of your stories is probably true. Things'll go a lot worse for you if I talk."

"And we'll tell the cops about them if you ever come after us," Sally added. She snatched the keys from Ida and dropped them into the trunk. "I'm leaving you the car keys – if you want them. The plan was to throw them into the corn but it's better if you get away from here fast. I trust it won't take you long to get from the trunk into the backseat. You might wanna think about stealing another car first opportunity; this purple monster will be all over the news."

The lid was slammed shut. Sally went to the driver's side front door, opened it, wiped off the gun and left it on the Capri's front seat. She didn't want to even be around the thing. The knife she'd brought was heaved into the field.

Louis listened intently and struggled to comprehend how someone who adored him, who looked up to him, could do this. For someone with so much experience of being metaphorically knifed in the back, with such finely honed senses about it, his lack of perception was startling.

It would take him hours to grasp that he hadn't convinced Ida to help him rob a bank, as he'd smugly thought, but that she'd had her own agenda.

He would never fully grasp that Ida's actions had little to do with the money – she'd been set to get half as it was. She'd decided to participate, even go to jail, for the chance to humiliate him, to use him, and then abandon him. There was a certain poetry at work.

22.

we dumped him in the trunk

Sally's car was parked a kilometre away, back in Carmel, two blocks from the credit union, on a side street.

The plan, as agreed to the night before in a clandestine phone call, was for Sally to leave her car where it wouldn't be remarked on. She would then walk along the side of the road in the dark of early morning, dodge into the bush if a car approached, then hide herself at the rendezvous spot until Louis and Ida arrived there after the robbery.

Things had gone according to plan except for the moment when Louis almost ran over her with the Civic where she was crouched among the corn stalks.

With Ida driving, the pair now headed toward Carmel and Sally's car. The Civic would be left on the street, the incriminating evidence in the trunk pitched into a garbage can.

Somewhere, not far behind them, a police cruiser rounded a bend. It was visible in Ida's rear-view mirror, but she didn't notice.

The two officers inside the speeding car had heard a radio report about the Carmel Credit Union robbery. They were speeding to the bank and looking out for a late model purple car. Two male suspects. Armed and dangerous.

The escalating wail soon caused both Ida and Sally to desperately search their mirrors.

"Oh my god no! It's a police car! What do I do now?" begged Ida, her voice quivering badly.

With the cruiser getting closer, Officer Jobe cursed at the driver of the little silver Civic ahead for not pulling over to the shoulder.

"Women fucking drivers," said his partner, head craned forward, peering intently.

Sally took her eyes from the side mirror – watching the cop car – to glance at her friend. What was Ida doing? She was in a trance. Mystified, Sally looked down at the shoulder of the highway. It was narrow and dropped off steeply towards a ditch, which was maybe why Ida hadn't pulled over.

Ahead on the right was a gravel road.

"There! There!" Sally pointed. "Slow down and turn onto that road!"

Ida made no movement. They were almost at the road.

"Go! Go!" Sally yelled, waving her hand toward the right. "Ida! Right! Go! Go!"

Ida came to life with a spasm on hearing the yelled commands. She heard the injunction to turn and saw Sally's hand maniacally waving in the direction of a road. Abruptly, Ida jammed on the brakes, swung the steering wheel violently rightward and slewed the Civic around the corner. Dust flew as the car slid sideways. After she'd managed to straighten it, she floored it again, showering pebbles behind her.

"What the fuck," said Officer Jobe as his cruiser sailed past Ida and the dirt road. He slammed on his brakes and fishtailed forward. When the cruiser came to a stop he put it in reverse.

"No! No! No!" screamed Sally. "Stop the car for chrissakes! Stop!"

Once again, Ida stood on her brakes. Like she had first discovered as a young baseball player with a runner on third: at her moments of greatest confusion she obeyed orders without understanding them.

As the women's car slid to a stop in the middle of the dirt road, the police cruiser pulled up behind them. One cop was on the radio calling in their position while the other, head down, was scrambling to get behind his open door, weapon in hand.

Ida looked wildly about, tears welling.

"Listen sweetie," said Sally firmly. "We have to tell them we were returning the money. Okay?"

"What?"

"When the cops ask you about the robbery tell them how Louie forced you to rob the bank, just like you practiced, and tell them we dumped him in the trunk of the Capri so we could take the money back. Okay?"

Ida stared forward.

"Okay Ida?"

"Okay."

The pair sat for two silent minutes basking in self-recrimination, afraid to move while the officers waited for back up.

"Sally," said Ida.

"Yes, sweetie?"

"What you said makes no sense. Won't the police just say that I should have called to tip them off about the robbery so they could step in instead of going through with it and getting you to help me return the money?"

Sally could hear a second police car, siren screaming, getting nearer. "Okay, you're right. Tell them you didn't call the cops because you didn't want to turn Louie in. Fuck, you used to tell me how much you loved him. You can go to town on that. Tell them the plan was to let the robbery go ahead and then return the money, so no one would know who took it, and you could only do that by waiting till you could get Louie's gun off him and get the money away from him."

"And I needed you for that."

"Yes. And tell them you didn't pull over for the cop car because the shoulder was too narrow."

The women clasped hands, but only briefly, because by then the cops outside were yelling at them to show their hands and get out of the car.

23.

he took the hatchet down to the river

Grief stricken, Reg sat on his haunches and cried most of the night.

At daybreak, he'd tried to face Lawrence's corpse. It was an unbearable scene. Very bloody. Reg couldn't do it.

An hour later he rallied, got near the body, but kept his face turned away except for one quick glance to locate the handle of the hatchet. He pulled on it; a repulsive act because the resistance insisted that this was a real body, now reduced to a piece of meat. But it was something he had to do. Reg had formulated a plan and it was imperative to remove any trace of himself from the scene.

He took the hatchet down to the river and scrubbed it clean. He wiped it dry on his jacket. When he got back to the truck he threw it on the floor of the cab.

Before leaving, he returned to Lawrence's body and apologized for the thousandth time.

A few minutes later, Reg drove off in the pickup.

He was heading home. He planned to stash the bags of smokes in the cabin on his family's property before taking the truck back to Lawrence's.

It would take all his courage to go into the cabin but it was the one spot on their land that his old man never bothered with. And because he kept an eye on Reg, he knew that his son never went near the place either.

The cabin was referred to as the 'outside bedroom' because his sister used to have sleepovers there. Thirteen-year-old girls with an eight-year-old Reg sneaking up to the window to listen to incomprehensible talk about things that bored him.

He'd tried a sleepover, on his own, a month or so later, but he'd been awakened by a bear scratching at the door. His night of terror had left him afraid to even enter the place after that— and permanently terrified of bears.

"Did any bears come around?" his sister had slyly asked next morning, "They always do." And Reg had found confirmation of the menace of bears rather than the truth of what had happened.

With the smokes stashed in the cabin, Reg took the truck back to Lawrence's. He hoped that Lawrence's brother and his girlfriend weren't around so that when they saw the truck they would assume that Lawrence had returned it and then left with someone else.

It was close. Just after he'd gotten out of the truck, keys in hand, Reg heard a car turn into the long curving drive. He dove for cover and was pretty certain that he hadn't been seen.

He made his way through the bush to the road and began his walk of a few kilometres to get back home. When the body was discovered it would give the impression that his friend had gone to the river in someone else's car and that would divert suspicion away from him since he was carless.

It was a good scheme, Reg decided. "I should have been a cop," he thought, "I can think like a criminal."

24.

lady luck was back on his side, cozying up

It took five minutes of pounding a rhythmic tattoo with his feet for Louis to break into the back seat of the Capri. Fuck! Fuck! Fuck! Every kick had been accompanied by a curse at Ida and Sally.

As he drove up onto the highway he knew that a description of the purple car would by now be all over the police radios. It was best to avoid the highway as much as possible; it's where the cops would focus. Get on a back road. The cops didn't have enough cars to cover them all.

So much for fucking luck.

Louis cursed his own arrogance; thinking that he could steal and drive such a noticeable vehicle without getting caught. It was like he had some secret wish to go to prison. He'd have to think about that possibility sometime.

He drove southeast on the highway, turned left on the first secondary road he saw, staying to the speed limit, and regained some degree of calm. The emotional storm of anger at Sally and Ida had largely blown itself out. The women had launched a personal attack but there was a certain elegance in what they'd done; even he could appreciate that.

East for two kilometres, then south on another secondary road running parallel to the highway. He doubted this decision at first but then told himself it was a good one. He had a knack for impulsively choosing the right escape option.

As a teenager, Louis and a couple of friends had jumped the back alley fence at a lumber supply yard and set off an alarm. They were screwing about, climbing on the woodpiles, when a police car squealed up in front. The three boys booted it over the back fence. His cronies went left and he went right, past the back of a Costco and then down another alley. The cops had swung around the lumber yard and into the alley just in time to grab Louis's two friends who had chosen the wrong direction. Louis, meanwhile, walked to a main street, went into a corner diner because it looked to offer some security, and came across a friend of his father's on his way out the door. The guy drove him home. The police, slowly trolling by, saw him but did nothing. This kid was with his dad so obviously not the one they were looking for. As things turned out, his pals wouldn't give up his name, but because the crime was so minimal they were never pushed particularly hard about it. Louis was lucky like that about impulsive decisions.

He now recognized the road he was on, having been over it that morning. It led directly to Larry's. It appeared that lady luck was back at his side, cozying up.

Louis saw the flashing red light moving speedily towards him, and he heard the siren. He was stopped at an intersection where his secondary road crossed over the highway. The cruiser was coming from his left. "Shit," he whispered aloud. Clearly he and his purple car were not going to be able to avoid being seen.

And they were seen, but unbeknownst to Louis, the cops speeding by had just gotten a radio report that the two bank robbery suspects were being held south of Carmel. The arresting officers needed back up, immediately, so this particular cruiser had been directed to head north from its detachment. The officer saw the purple car but wasn't interested, thinking it was likely the purple car seen in the vicinity of the Carmel Credit Union that had wrongly been identified as belonging to the robbers.

Louis watched the cruiser pass and followed it for a long time with his eyes. He knew it would make a u-turn at any moment. Maybe three seconds. One, two, three, he counted. He wasn't going to try to flee when they returned. A car chase was not his style. The police car passed from view.

Five, six, seven… Nothing. He advanced through the intersection and drove the rest of the way back to Larry's house.

Louis made his way up the driveway, not spotting Reg who as he climbed out of the cab of the Larry's pickup. Louis was surprised to see the vehicle, parked in a novel spot at the end of the house.

After parking the Capri inside the garage, he wiped it down.

In spite of a thorough search of the house, Larry was nowhere to be found. Louis set about carefully wiping down the house; everything that he and Ida may have touched.

In the kitchen he found a set of keys for the truck.

As he drove it out of the yard, Louis stole a glance at the gas gauge. Three quarter's full. Nice. Leave it to Larry.

The plan to hole up at Larry's for a few days, till the cops gave up searching for him and Ida, had gone out the window. Louis's new plan consisted of getting back to the city and confronting Ida and Sally.

Louis saw a hatchet on the floor of the passenger side and shoved it under the seat. The last thing he needed would be for someone to walk by him when he was stopped somewhere and see it, some nosey parker who would call the cops.

"Sorry for stealing your truck Larry," he whispered under his breath as he headed for home.

25.

let's hope the cells aren't framed with two-by-fours

It was nearly nine PM when Schmidt and Wilde, two provincial police detectives from down south, arrived at the local detachment. The place was a modified bungalow out on the highway, and was typically closed in the evening.

"Jesus," Wilde whispered as an aside, as the two walked up the wooden steps, "let's hope the cells aren't framed with two-by-fours and covered with drywall."

They knew the constable on duty, joked a bit and got some background on the day's events, but the detectives knew the basics already. The two women they had come to pick up were in the holding cells.

"Cells? As in plural?" asked Wilde.

"Yes sir."

"Is there an interview room here?"

"Between the cells."

"That's good," said Wilde. "So they've had no communication with each other?"

"No," he was assured, and the constable added that the detachment had been laid out the way it was for just that reason. He said it with pride.

"So you wanna interview them before you take them?" the constable asked, looking from one detective to the other, pleased, hopeful this would lead to some overtime.

"Yeah," lead detective Schmidt interjected, "before they have a chance to work on a story. Sorry 'bout that. I know you want to get home to bed."

Schmidt: Please state your name.
Ida: Ida Finger.
Schmidt: You are here on suspicion of bank robbery. Do you...
Ida: Can I get a Tylenol? My head's pounding from stress.
Schmidt: I'll see what I can do. You are...
Ida: Sally had nothing to do with this. And where is she?
Schmidt: Playing cards in her cell.

Ida: She's innocent. She was only helping me return the money.

Schmidt: And what money would that be?

Ida: From the credit union.

Schmidt: Well, that's a good start. Things will go very smoothly with your co-operation. Do you admit then that you robbed the Carmel Farmer's Co-operative Credit Union this morning?

Ida: Yes.

Schmidt: And you were with another person...

Ida: Louis.

Schmidt: Louis?

Ida: Louis Henderson.

Schmidt looked down at the notes he'd made when he was called, and read that the recording from the credit union's camera didn't help to determine whether the robbers who'd snatched the money were men or not. The question had come up because the staff said that the one with a gun was a man (masculine voice) but the accomplice may have been a woman (although he/she was dressed like a man). Schmidt jotted a further note: '*Assume that one or both women pretended to be male. Check to see if either has any theatrical training in her background.*'

Schmidt: And where is Louis now?

Ida: We locked him in a trunk.

Schmidt: A car trunk?

Ida: Yes. I managed to sneak a call to Sally last night. She's my friend. I told her...

Schmidt: Whoa, whoa, whoa. You said you robbed the credit union...

Ida: Louis forced me...

Schmidt: Okay, leave that for now, we need to go through this so I understand.

Ida: But he forced me! The bastard. It's not fair. Why should he get off?

Ida began to cry so Schmidt held off with the questions for

a couple of minutes while she composed herself. He looked about, saw a crucifix on the wall and wondered what its purpose was. To suggest that confession was good for the soul maybe? To make people feel guilty? Make them think of God? Or maybe that they were going to everlastingly burn in hell if they didn't come clean?

Schmidt: I'm going to ask some questions. I just want, for now, to get an overview of what happened.

Ida: Okay.

Schmidt: So you say you robbed the credit union with this Louis Henderson.

Ida: Yes. He forced me…

Schmidt: How did he force you?

Ida: He held a gun on me.

Schmidt: Okay, so you helped him rob the credit union and then the two of you left in a car.

Ida: Right.

Schmidt: What sort of car?

Ida: A purple Capri. We…

Schmidt: Wait. What happened to the Capri?

Ida: We switched it in the cornfield.

Schmidt: For the Civic?

Ida: Yes.

Schmidt: How did the Civic get there?

Ida: Louis stole it yesterday and stashed it there this morning.

Schmidt: And now he's in the trunk of the Capri.

Ida: Yes.

Schmidt: Tell me how that happened.

Ida: Sally drove north this morning and hid at the spot where the Civic was waiting. I phoned her last night and set it up. When we got back to the cars we forced Louis into the trunk. Then we headed for the bank to return the money.

Schmidt: To return… I don't understand. If you had a phone, why didn't you just call the police?

Ida: (Pause) I didn't want it to be known that Louis was involved in the robbery. I still care about him in spite or everything. So I was going to return the money. Hide it. Then

117

make an anonymous call and tell the bank where the money was.

In the next few days Ida was bright enough to realize she was less likely to get tripped up if she stayed with the simple stories concocted with Sally and Louis.

Schmidt made a note to the effect that for someone who didn't want her lover to go to jail Ida seemed pretty anxious now to sell him out. '*Suggests there is no Louis,*' he wrote. His gut was telling him that once all the evidence was in, that it would show that the two who'd staged the robbery were the women now in custody.

Schmidt: Where's the car with Louis in the trunk?

After Ida gave the location of where she'd last seen the Capri, Schmidt nodded to Wilde who got up and left the room.

Schmidt: Okay, let's go back to the beginning. Tell me about how Louis came to force you to rob a bank and what his plan was.
Ida: Sure. Louis called me three days ago and asked me to go fishing with him. He's an old boyfriend so I said yes to get out of town.
Schmidt: You were at home?
Ida: Yes, at my apartment.

Schmidt got the address, confirmed that Ida lived alone, and jotted a note that he saw no reason to search her apartment as a matter of urgency since they had the money and a confession. And this Louis Henderson – if he existed – was supposedly locked in a car trunk.

Schmidt: So he didn't force you to go with him?
Ida: Not to leave with him, no.
Schmidt: Okay, I understand. Continue.
Ida: So we drove north all day.
Schmidt: And did you stay at a motel?

Ida: No. We were going to stay at his grandma's but she told us to leave. So we slept in the car.

Schmidt: Where's his grandmother's house?

Ida: I don't know the name of the place.

Schmidt: You went there but you don't know where it is?

Ida: It was night and I was sleeping beforehand.

Schmidt: Okay. Please continue.

Ida: The next day we drove to Larry's place – that's Louis's brother – and we stayed there.

Schmidt: And where's that?

Ida: I don't know. I was sleeping when we got there.

Schmidt: But you drove away from the place during the day…

Ida: We took circuitous routes and Louis was driving. Even when we got the second car and I drove back, I only followed Louie's directions.

Schmidt: You were driving the second car and you didn't make any effort to get away?

Ida: He was right behind me and he had a gun don't forget. And he had my phone.

There was a pause and then Schmidt asked for Louis's address, which Ida provided. It wasn't in the city.

Schmidt: Louis Henderson. The name sounds familiar.

Ida: He was a heavy metal singer when he was young.

She provided a name of the band but Schmidt had never heard of them. So this is one of these groupies who thinks they're in a relationship with a rock star or a movie star, he thought.

Ida: This wasn't his first crime. I can give you the details of at least five more he told me about. Serious crimes. They'll show you the sort of person we're talking about.

26.

Hendrix was dead

Louis was forty kilometres from the city when he pulled off
the highway and drove slowly along a gently winding road
that bordered the park-like campus of a community college. It
was an oasis of mostly lawns and walking paths. Probably
once an estate.

Fuck he was tired. Long long day, and he hadn't slept the
night before. His plan to chase down Ida and Sally could wait
a few hours. All he wanted now was to find a place to park,
somewhere out of sight of the road, and take a long nap.

The problem was that the college parking lots were
massive and almost empty. Within an hour or two, when the
buildings were locked up, any vehicle still parked there
would draw the attention of campus security.

He slowed down when he spotted a cluster of several cars
parked immediately on his right, a long way from any college
buildings.

He stopped Larry's pick-up on the side of the road. Across
from him, and the cars, was an old brick house sitting all by
itself amid forest. He turned off the motor and studied the
place. He assumed the house was part of the college and that
the parked cars belonged to people who were visiting the
place but using the college lot because there were two cars in
the house's driveway, leaving no room for more. If his truck
was parked in the lot with the others, it would go unnoticed.
Even if the other vehicles left, and the truck was there by
itself, security would assume the driver was in the house and
wouldn't bother checking him out.

After parking, he got out of the truck and looked about for
a place to take a leak.

A faint trace of twilight lingered, allowing him to see the
bush surrounding the house across the road.

He crossed over and was walking past the house when he
heard a man's voice.

"Hi." The speaker was obscured by shadows that draped
over the front steps.

"Hi," Louis said, stopping. "Just takin' a little walk, headin' for the bush. Nature's callin'. Hope that's okay."

"Not a problem. You look a bit familiar."

Shit, Louis thought, he was standing here, draped in illumination from the side door light; not the way to remain incognito. "I get that sometimes," he said.

"Didn't you used to be in a band?"

No answer.

"Were you in God's Gift to Women?"

"Yeah."

"God! GGW. I saw them at Copps Coliseum." It sounded more like a personal rebuke than the usual fan recollection. "Me and my friends. So you're…"

"Louis Henderson."

"Louis Henderson, the singer." The tone conveyed something like contempt.

Louis didn't like the inflection; he got that sometimes too, people denying their youth, passing off their past interest as immaturity. He never challenged those sorts. The band had come out of the arts scene but he couldn't argue their legitimacy without sounding pretentious. He yawned.

"You tired?" The disembodied voice asked.

"Yeah, been driving all day. I just need to take a leak and then a little walk to wake up." He began to inch forward, signalling an end to the conversation.

"Come inside." The voice was missing the usual enthusiasm of the devoted fan. It added, "I have a bit of a party going on for my students. You might like it. Lots of your fans here. And a bathroom." The word 'fans' sounded vaguely contemptuous.

Louis was tempted by the idea. A place to sit down, food, alcohol. But he hesitated. He didn't like the guy because of the superiority vibe. "Okay," he said, fatigue weighing in.

The man stood as Louis approached the steps, and extended his hand. "I'm Clark."

The shadowy figure, so far as Louis could make out, was close to forty, older than what he would have assumed from the voice. Louis followed him through the front entranceway and immediately dove for the bathroom just inside the door.

Shortly thereafter, as he trailed Clark down the hallway that ran through the centre of the dimly lit house, Louis saw a cluster of several young people in the living room ahead. Most were standing. It seemed a pretty tame affair with the music and voices both low. The creaking from his footsteps on the old floor was louder than the get-together.

Despite looking down on GGW, with requisite academic distain, Clark was not above announcing Louis to the assembly in a smarmy tone, simultaneously getting the credit for dragging in a celebrity while showing his distaste for such low brow music.

The group's socializing immediately halted. A rock star had just entered their midst. This was special. A few people whispered explanations to those who'd never heard of GGW. Several bright-cheeked young people formed an admiring cluster around their guest, shaking his hand and welcoming him. They made room for him on a love seat.

Seated, Louis found himself still surrounded by the group of smiling young people; warmed by their proximity to this sun. He began to feel the weight of celebrity and exhaustion laying on his shoulders.

Voices took turns reciting Louis Henderson anecdotes – stories that Louis never wanted to hear again – but he feigned interest indulgently.

"So Hendrix took some of Louis's stuff," someone said, "and when they asked him why he thought Hendrix had taken it, Louis said, 'He did it to feed his slavish imitation of me'." Everyone laughed.

Louis blushed. Hendrix? As if he ever imitated anyone. Plus Hendrix was dead by the time GGW was active. He didn't remember who the story was actually about, doubted it even happened, but remembered that Louis Henderson, as he was at that time, liked issuing pithy quotes.

Another student filled a gap between stories with an aside to Louis about why he thought his music had been so popular. "Beginning with the sexually aggrandizing name, you were obviously a precursor of hip-hop."

Louis wasn't sure what the guy was on about and didn't ask for clarification. He skimmed over the sea of words that followed, like a sailboat over calm water.

The demands from being the centre of attention, combined with three whiskey sours, soon left him wondering if there were bedrooms upstairs and if so, would he be allowed to stay the night. He glanced at Clark, sitting beside him on the love seat, who was studying him imperiously, perhaps quizzically, as if Louis was a specimen and there was something unpleasant about him.

Most of the students, quickly bored with celebrity, turned away. Their voices becoming serious.

The word 'suicide' was soon being bandied about.

Fuck, Louis thought. It always went back to the suicides.

At one of his concerts a guy had stabbed himself during a song about suicide – apparently to punish the girlfriend who'd just dumped him. It was shocking, and headline news.

Then another guy slashed his own throat – for unknown reasons – during the group's next concert. This was followed by a self-stabbing suicide at the next concert.

Suicide had become a fad at GGW concerts. A sort of mass psychosis. The band, it was said, was a reflection of the loneliness and despair of their generation.

Louis never understood the deaths or why the band was being blamed for them. He pleaded for no more suicides but it didn't stop them.

Breaking up the band was the only way to end it he told reporters at the press conference when GGW was dissolved.

After that, the name of Louis Henderson was held in high moral regard – for a few days anyway – until he was approached by paparazzi on the street. He'd talked for a while then said, "Don't ask me any more questions," whereupon he was immediately asked a question about one of the dead kids. Instead of answering sympathetically, Louis pushed his way through the crowd, saying "Let it go!"

He'd only been talking about ending this particular line of questioning, and his harassment, not saying that it was time to dismiss any concern for those who had died, but the press painted it differently. 'Indifference', it was called, 'callousness', and he was vilified as an unfeeling prick.

"It was all so sad," Louis said, in response to a question

from one one of Clark's guests.

He stood up, and wanted to run. It was always the way.

"Excuse me," he said to the group, "I need to rest. I'm beat."

He sat back down and looked at Clark who smiled back, exuding superiority again, like he knew something the others didn't.

Louis closed his eyes. After twenty minutes, he was asleep, tilting to the right, his head on Clark's shoulder.

27.

Saturday: all of the mobster courage he could muster

It was going on for three AM when Keith planted his right foot immediately beside the trap door. His left leg was extended like a sprinter's, for heft, but it kept sliding on the undergrowth. Still, with both hands gripping the door, he managed to slowly inch it upwards until achieving a perfectly upright position. Precarious, but the thing looked and felt wide and heavy enough to stay in place.

Crouching, listening, Keith inserted his head through the opening and looked towards the dully lit passageway leading to the lab. The battleship grey (or perhaps, submarine grey, given the underground location) floor and walls shimmered faintly. About three metres along, the barren tunnel curved to the right.

Keith sat up and turned his attention back to the matter at hand. He gripped the head of the steel ladder, considered, reconsidered, eased his foot down onto the top step, and finally began descending.

Keith had been drawn back here to the Hayes farm, in the middle of the night, by an irresistible compulsion. He had to know if there was a body still out in the field. Since there'd been nothing on the news, he was convinced that the cops hadn't bothered following up on his call to Crime Stoppers. On finding nothing, he'd gotten the bright idea that the body might have, or rather must have, been put below ground via the opening he'd previously observed. His curiosity was overwhelming.

It had taken all of the mobster courage he could muster to plant that first foot on the ladder. The rest wasn't much easier. With mouse-like quiet and timidity, he reached the floor of the tunnel and paused with a hand on one of the ladder's rungs. It was a lifeline tying him to some solidity. He wiped the sweat from the palm of his free hand, on the front of his shirt, switched hands, and did the same for the other. Drawing on his steely mobster reserve he eventually cut the umbilical and inched along the tunnel, pausing at the bend. A poster taped to the wall, of a topless model dressed like a firefighter, shocked him into stopping. He'd translated the sight of a human form into the idea that here was a real person. Once past that misconception he gently edged his face around the turn of the tunnel. In the distance, a ceiling light was on and the steel table in the middle of the lab was clearly visible.

A shape on the floor to the right of the table, laying in its shadow, drew his attention. It might be a body.

Keith stared, unwilling to move or look away, trying to determine for certain what the thing was by its shape. What gradually materialized was a person with an enormous head, but on second thought no, it wasn't a big head, it was a head with a halo of long blonde hair strewn over the person's back. And then, just as suddenly, Keith realized that the shape was moving, expanding and contracting: breathing. The figure coughed, adjusted itself, stretched an arm, and a book fell from its hand.

Involuntarily, Keith recoiled, turned and fled back up the tunnel and the ladder, almost noiselessly. He had the presence of mind to recognize that a closed trapdoor would slow any potential pursuit, so he wrestled it shut.

Just as he was straightening up he saw a light, the bobbing and darting beam of a flashlight, through the trees behind the barn.

He ran. Got over the fence.

Keeping low, he scooted across the field, stumbling over furrows. Soon he was at the fence by the road. Went over it on the fly.

When he eventually slowed to a walk, certain he was on his own, his thoughts went back to the figure he'd seen sleeping on the floor of the tunnel. Long blonde hair. In all likelihood, he thought, this was the guy the cops were looking for in the case of Stonewall Cutter, Lemony something-or-other. He certainly matched the description that had been given on the news.

28.

driving a convertible with a chimpanzee in the passenger seat

At six AM Louis awoke to find himself alone, still on the love seat, his head now tilted back. He'd been dreaming that he was pissing blood and enough was enough. Before sitting up, he lay still for a minute in order to mentally test for pursuers. Nothing.

No one was stirring in the house. The floorboards loudly crunched in the stillness as he walked down the hall.

He glanced into the outside darkness through the kitchen window before entering the bathroom, and saw two cars still parked in the lot across the road, illuminated within the amber circle cast by the lamp atop a high pole. Not everyone had left. Presumably there were other couches or beds upstairs – or maybe the college teacher had guests in his.

Louis left the house, quietly, not wanting to root around in the kitchen and make yet more noise. He would get some coffee along the way. His stomach growled despite the promissory note.

Back at the truck, he discovered a parking ticket stuck under the driver's-side wiper blade. Laughing softly, he dropped it on the ground and climbed into the cab. A short time later he merged Larry's pickup into the early morning commute, turned on the radio he'd been too preoccupied to think of the night before, twisted the dial, and stopped at the first radio station offering a respite from loud static. A jazz trio filled the cab with sound.

He laid out a course of action. First head to Ida's, confront her, and get his share of the money. He was magnanimous, and would take only what had been agreed upon. Let bygones be bygones. The possibility that Ida would again threaten to expose him if he showed up at her apartment didn't worry him in the least; he could give a rat's ass. She'd give him the money. End of story. If she wasn't home he would tear her place apart until he found it. And if that still didn't turn it up then he'd head for Sally's and do the same thing there – those two were lucky he wasn't a violent sort – and if the money wasn't at Sally's he'd find out where this boyfriend of Ida's lived and head there.

Ida. How could the woman have been so stupid? Didn't she know he'd come after her? The robbery had gone flawlessly, so far as he was concerned, and they had walked away with no trouble. It showed how things could work out for her if she stuck with him. It had to have been Sally who talked her into the double-cross. He felt hurt by Ida's betrayal and basked in his injured feelings. The bank robbery was done for her alone and this was how she repaid him. Louis shook his head sadly at the fickleness of women.

The news came on the radio at the top of the hour. After some international stories, the announcer turned to local matters. "Police are still searching for Lawrence Boissoneault who goes by the street name of Lemony," the announcer said. "Boissoneault is wanted as a person of interest in the death of eighteen-year-old Stonewall Cutter last Sunday night. Cutter's death was originally given as suicide but is now being treated as a murder. It was the third in the city this year. Boissoneault is thirty-two years old, white, with a long blonde ponytail and a large tattoo of T. S. Eliot on his neck. There's a picture of him on our website. He's a member of the Tricep Motorcycle Club. Police stressed that Boissoneault is not a suspect."

There had been a jerk of recognition at the news and Louis's driving speed slowed to a crawl while his thoughts raced. A line of cars was soon building behind him so he pulled into a donut store parking lot and sat while the truck idled.

Louis's emotions slowly imploded. Stonewall Cutter was his son.

This was what it had come to. Stone, so far as he knew, was living in Winnipeg. He'd obviously come back home, but to the city rather that to his grandparent's estate, for excitement perhaps, maybe to find his father. He must have gotten involved with the Triceps and things had ended horribly.

Louis stewed in his own little hell. He should have

protected his son. This was his fault.

The previous year Louis had related a story about his past to Ida.

"When Stone was born," Louis said, "I was often on the road with GGW. I'd stayed pretty clean durin' those times, but after the suicides at our concerts, and the disbanding of the group, I lost myself in drugs. Still, I put on a show. Still the immature dude who thinks fame will give him the love and attention he lacks. I have a photo of myself from those days, driving a convertible with a chimpanzee in the passenger seat. The bon vivant, retired rock star. It was all false. The wife, Daisy, saw my antics as indifference and selfishness. She said that the marriage was over. Maybe it was for the best. I couldn't look after myself; what could I offer a family?" Indeed, besides his sports car, all that he owned was a small suitcase, and its contents consisted of one change of clothes and a pair of jean-shorts with a ripped crotch.

Louis went on to say that he wanted to continue seeing Stone but Daisy wanted him out of their son's life until he cleaned up his act. Her lawyer had a letter delivered to him that said as much. That was about twelve years ago.

The evening he received the letter was the last time that Louis had seen Stone.

He remembered that night well, he told Ida. After reading the lawyer's letter, he'd headed for the compound (a big gated house, with guards, where his wife lived with her wealthy father).

There was some sort of party going on. It was an upscale affair. People showing off their expensive fashions. For some reason, Louis said, he still recalled a dude dressed to look like Nat King Cole. And a rock star who was walking around with an entourage of blondes. And he saw his father-in-law locked in an embrace with a young Harlow type.

"I shoulda gotten someone to take a picture – God knows there were enough cameras around. I would have if I'd known what was to come – and then used it for leverage. Daisy's old man saw me and had his aides throw me out. Told me to never come back. To forget about Stone and Daisy. He said, 'We're gonna follow your movements. Watch you. And if we ever see you again, kill you'."

"So," Louis said, "I left. I believed the old guy. He was a grifter who paid off the mob and politicians in the city for favours, and had no doubt put out some hits on people."

And so, Louis's father-in-law became one more thing to put in his rear-view mirror, and to constantly check on to make sure it wasn't creeping up on him.

An hour later, Louis, still sitting in the parked vehicle at the donut shop, started the truck and put it into drive.

He had made two adjustments to his plans.

First, he was going to pick up Joseph. For three years, since meeting in the psych hospital, they'd been buddies. As far as father-son relationships went, his relationship with Joseph was the closest he'd ever come. Although his treatment of the kid hadn't been all bad, by any means, he was in no mood for self-forgiveness. He had never taken on any responsibility for Joseph; just picked him up when he wanted company. Only the week before he'd dropped him on the sidewalk near the hospital – practically kicked him out of the car – and driven away. Louis felt brought to his knees by this further guilt. What kind of fucking friend does that? From now on he was going to do everything he could for Joseph.

His second adjustment involved Jack Hayes.

Stone had apparently come to the city and met up with the Triceps. Louis knew they were connected to Jack Hayes; a dealer in drugs, prostitution, and whatever else the piece of shit figured he could make a buck at these days. Louis had chummed with him when they were in their early teens. They'd even gotten into some minor trouble with the cops. Louis avoided him after Jack started proposing more serious crimes. Now the fucker was killing kids. He'd always been a heartless bastard but this was a new low. How did anyone sink to that level – even Jack?

Louis was going to find Jack Hayes. He was going to terrorize him. He would hurt him, debase him, smash every bone in his body and then kill him as an act of mercy.

29.

I don't know a lot about art but I think it's ridiculing men

Schmidt had been surprised by the sheer amount of data on Louis Henderson available on the internet. The guy had a bad boy reputation. Frequent references to a 'troubled youth' but few specifics.

One story alleged that Henderson had been expelled from university for cheating. Apparently he'd been enrolled in some film course but attended few classes and saw none of the films they were studying. When it was time for the exam he hired an actor who'd been an extra in one of the films to take the exam. The presumption being, apparently, that the guy would have something of interest to say about the film. It was so stupid it was laughable.

"Whoa!" Schmidt said suddenly, stopping at a head and chest photo of a woman in a black niqab staring directly at the camera, her left hand held down the right side of her dress, exposing a breast. A twenty-something Louis looked to be nursing at it. The photo was included in a column called *There You Go* and the gist of the article was about the controversy the photo had stirred. *'I wanted to play with the mother image and role,'* the photog was quoted as saying.

'Is this sexual empowerment or porn?' the columnist asked Louis, and he replied, *'It's neither. You're missing the point. It's ridiculing grown men for feeding off women to survive. They cover up women thinking they can control them like property but are subject to their sexual power and their power over life.'*

Schmidt shrugged, he didn't get it. Henderson sounded more serious than he would have given him credit for. The woman did have a nice rack though.

The detective was looking at Ida.

She sat silently as if the two were trying to wait each other out. Their second meeting, back at Central, had gone into detail about Ida's alleged kidnapping and coercion, and the interactions with the family of Louis Henderson. Schmidt had checked them out.

Ida: It's not fair. I love Louie but he took advantage of me!

His superiors had always held up Schmidt's interviews as textbook and he thought of that now. This was being recorded and he imagined an instructor in police college some day speaking over a video of the interview, 'Remember, time is his ally. No need to bully people. Watch how he breaks down her story that a man was involved. He doesn't browbeat the suspect, just shows her the inevitability of her story falling apart.'
Schmidt shuffled through some papers. Eventually he continued.

Schmidt: I'm sorry, there's no getting around it. We're trying to confirm your story but there are problems. For one thing, you said that you stopped at the home of Louis Henderson's grandmother. Both of Louis Henderson's grandmothers are dead.
Ida: I don't understand.
Schmidt: And you said this woman said she was going to call 9-1-1, but no such call was made that night by anyone in the area.

Another long silence ensued while Ida struggled to keep her composure. And again, Schmidt was patient.

Ida: So who was the old lady?
Schmidt: Are you sure there was one?
Ida: Yes there was. Fuck! I told you! She threw us off her property... You know, maybe she wasn't his birth grandmother, maybe just someone he called 'grandma'. It sounded like she'd raised him so she might have taken him in as a kid... That makes sense. She looks too young to be his grandmother.

Schmidt appeared to be in pain but made a note and indicated he would look into it.

132

Schmidt: And the brother? The family said he's dead.

Ida: Louie told me he was dead but then said that was wrong. So he's really dead?

Schmidt: Yes.

He didn't elaborate. It was more complicated than that. They'd been advised that Larry had been found dead in Uruguay where he'd been smuggling drugs, but when asked what they'd done with the body, the government said they couldn't figure out what happened to it.

Ida: Louis said the brother had nothing to do with the family, so it makes sense that he's still alive. They tried to have him put away so maybe he changed his name and faked his death.

Maybe you watch too many TV shows, thought Schmidt and pondered how much to say about Louis. Like the fact that his parents hadn't seen him in many years and said that he had disappeared and was maybe dead.

Schmidt: Louis Henderson closed a business a couple of years back, sold his house, but no one has any idea of where he went after that.

Ida: But Louis said… I thought he still lived in the same house. Of course the guy would lie about that, like he lied about everything else.

Schmidt: Makes it hard to confirm your story. It even makes your story problematic; that you're claiming to have been influenced by a man who's disappeared, and who may have died years ago for all we know.

Ida: Are you saying I had something to do with his disappearance? Like I killed him? Oh, for God's sake.

Silence.

Ida: You know, thinking about it, it would make sense if Louie's been using a false name. He was always worried about people chasing him.

Schmidt: Who did he say was chasing him?

Ida: He would never say. I thought it was the taxman or the co...the police, but it could have been the mob or maybe fans, and, you know, the Uruguayans.

Schmidt: Uruguayans?

Ida: He was always going on about them. They were enemies.

Schmidt: Everything will come out, Ida. That's a certainty. It's a question of whether we get your co-operation or not and getting it will always help you in the end.

Ida began to cry softly in frustration.

Ida: How many times do I have to tell you, I am co-operating? I don't care that he wasn't there in the trunk. That's where we left him. I swear!

Schmidt: But Ida, there wasn't even a car where you sent us! And there's much more than that that is problematic, as you know. We've looked into every one of the crimes you told us Louis committed and none of them checked out. Not one of them even happened.

Ida stared at the floor while Schmidt suppressed the urge to tell her that their investigation had confirmed that there was evidence that multiple cars had indeed been at the area of the rendezvous in the cornfield.

Ida: It is so unfair. He should have just left me alone. Now he's going to get off scot-free and I'm going to stay in jail.

Schmidt: We can't verify anything about him. Think of this from our perspective. It's like the guy no longer even exists. Or like he's gone into deep hiding.

The police investigation had also turned up that Ida's accomplice, Sally Potter, had been a very talented actress in her youth. Someone who could have been a professional. Someone who could convincingly portray a man.

134

30.

anybody have to have a go at you with the pliers

Jack Hayes returned home in the afternoon, still with no charges having been laid against him. He'd been in the hospital all week, getting treatment for his burned elbow.

Jaycee had started in on him while they were still in the car – about Lemony staying on at the farm – and after arriving home continued to go on about it. It was sure to bring trouble, she said. "You oughta tell him to leave. But you never listen to me." She stuck her nose in the air.

There were other guys who sometimes stayed at the farm to work in the lab or barn, and three of them were wanted on outstanding warrants, but Jaycee didn't raise these as issues, so it was apparent to Jack that Lemony's case was about something else. Maybe Lemony threatened Jaycee's spot in the pecking order around the farm, he thought. Sounded like guys listened to him and not her.

At first he'd been inclined to think that Lemony's situation, insofar as he understood it from Jaycee's account, was reason enough for the guy to have stayed on at the farm, and not a big deal, but Jack's highly developed sense of survival was now telling him differently.

Still though, he was making a concerted effort to not listen. Why the fuck didn't she shut up? He was loosing his patience. His elbow still hurt like hell because he was trying to hold off on the painkillers; they dulled his senses. This aggravation from Jaycee he could do without.

"Yeah, yeah, yeah, I hear you," he said, his voice rising. "Drop it!"

Jaycee knew when not to push further. She got up from the living room chair and went to the kitchen to bang pots and pans around as if she were performing some domestic chores. She sulked. She could do better than this guy and this place.

Jack climbed awkwardly up out of his chair, stopped in front of one of the high narrow windows, and stared down the long drive towards the front gate, imagining the processions of cops that had twice driven up the road in the last few days.

He went into the kitchen, rooted around on the bottom shelf of the fridge, came up with a package, opened it just enough to ascertain the contents, and went outside.

The collie was furiously lapping up water from a tin bowl, sending drops flying in a metre radius. On hearing the door, he bounded up on his hind legs and threw his front paws on Jack's chest.

Jack held the package off to the side while patting the dog with his other hand. "Stay down Rexie. Jesuz, you gotta fuckin' grow up." As he began down the porch steps, Rex piled into the side of his leg, determined to be the first to take that route. Jack was pushed against the railing and needed to grab hold to avoid going over. "Rex, you fuckin' psycho!"

The ever vigilant German Shepherd chained in front of the slaughterhouse gave a short yip that was suddenly cut short. He then stood dead still, likely with regret and some trepidation on realizing who he'd barked at. His ears were perked as he watched.

Jack didn't approach the dog. His directions to everyone were to keep the animal nasty so as to make him a better watchdog, and that meant never talking softly to him or petting him – as if any of his employees would have been stupid enough to try. Jack opened his package as he passed the dog and tossed the contents in its general direction. The collie headed for the thrown meat but a low guttural growl from the German Shepherd caused him to back off. Rex decided to follow his master instead.

Jack wadded the paper in his hand and noted that the grass he walked across had been recently cut. Looked good. Maybe done to impress him.

"You find any porcupines when I was gone Rexie, ya dumb mutt? Anybody have to have a go at you with the pliers?" The policy was to keep the collie in at night because he had a knack for finding trouble, but Jack couldn't know what had happened when he was in the hospital. Nobody was trustworthy.

There was no wind in this sheltered space between the house and the farm buildings, but overhead a sudden gust burst through the leaves of an oak tree, shoving them around like a bunch of toughs pushing their way through a crowd. Murmurs of dissent. Jack looked up at the sound.

"Bruce! Hey Chuck!" he called to the two guys dressed like members of Whistler's family who were working just inside the barn. They all shook hands and for the next ten minutes Jack grilled the pair with questions about not only the farm but the Ecstasy production that had just wrapped up.

"I understand Lemony's here," Jack said eventually.

"Yeah, he's down the hole cleanin' up," Bruce said, nodding in the direction of the always open hole in the floor that led to the lab below.

"There's some corn cobs in a box in the kitchen Chuckie," Jack said. "You wanna get them for the cows?"

"Yeah, sure." Chuck headed off, understanding that he was being sent away.

Jack and Bruce retreated toward the back of the barn where the latter retrieved an envelope and slipped it to Jack in a needlessly clandestine way.

Jack tucked it inside his shirt, thanked him, then headed for the basement lab. He stopped at the mouth of the tunnel, a metre below the barn floor, and contemplated the ridge where the metal plate had been positioned during the police raid. Oh, to put a weight on the plate, and on the one at the other end, outside. Trap Lemony inside. He would pound on the door but it would be ignored. He would discover the frustration of trying to open a door with no handle or key. A life lesson. Teach him it's always easier to get into something than to get out of it.

Jack sighed and climbed down the ladder, cursing profusely at the pain in his elbow.

Lemony looked up from where he was polishing the long stainless steel table in the centre of the room.

"Hey Fabio!" Jack said.

"Hey," Lemony answered, the unsaid word 'Dickhead' following in his thoughts.

"Where is everybody?"

"Gone home. Or out back, smoking."

"Ah."

After a few preliminaries about his elbow, Jack said, "Hear

the cops showed up looking for a body the other day."

"Yeah. Strange, eh? Didn't know what the fuck that was about, but, you know, something occurred to me after. Kenny was outside that night to take a leak and the dummy knocked himself unconscious."

"Where?"

"In the bush by the tunnel opening. I saw him struggling to get up when I went looking for him."

"And someone else was there?"

"Had to be. If they saw Kenny stretched out on the ground they could have thought he was dead and called the cops."

"And Kenny was unconscious so he doesn't know," Jack said, nodding. "We got security cameras all over the perimeter just for that reason, so's strangers aren't walkin' around the place. If they are, we got a big problem."

"True."

"I'm thinkin' this was the cops makin' somethin' up, so they could come back to the barn figurin' we'll have let our guard down, not expectin' two raids in one day."

"That makes sense too," Lemony pretended to agree.

"More sense than someone gettin' through our security." Jack looked quizzically at Lemony, as if waiting for a confession. "So what's this I hear about the cops lookin' for you?"

"I heard. I don't know what it's about."

"It's about some kid's murder is what I hear."

"That's what they said on the news but I don't even know the kid, never heard of him, so I don't know why they're looking for me."

"No?" Jack's eyebrows arched, creating something like the letter m across his forehead.

"Not so far as I know. That's why I stayed on here. I was hoping to get some more information."

"Sorry man, you can't do that."

Lemony wasn't about to argue. "Yes, I was expecting that. Jaycee…"

"Fuck Jaycee! I don't listen to that cunt. She's callin' for me to cut your balls off because she's pissed at you about somethin'. Maybe she blames you for the cops comin' here or

138

maybe for underminin' or embarrassin' her."

"Okay. I'll ask Bruce if he can give me a lift into town. Everybody's heading home today."

"No, you're not listenin'. I didn't say you had to go today. Did I say that? You can stay three nights and listen to the newscasts; see if this thing blows over or if it's somethin' you want to get out of town about. If you're still here in three days and the cops are still lookin' for you then, well that's too much heat on the farm. I'll want you to leave through the bush."

"Understood. Thanks."

Jack headed back towards the house. He wasn't about to put an envelope of money into the safe with Lemony in the room.

There was a bit of an additional swagger to his step as he went up the back porch stairs. He knew all about the murder of Stonewall Cutter and that Lemony had nothing to do with it, but he had played his part to perfection – acting like he was in the dark about what happened to the kid, and had no hand in his death.

31.

there's somethin' missin' in your brain

Keith had a key to Ida's apartment that she'd given him as an intimate gesture, a hopeful one, but Keith hadn't responded or understood. It was merely a matter of convenience, he thought. But it now had a more significant purpose. With the key he could spy on Ida and invade her privacy. She was now a notorious criminal so had suddenly become intensely desirable. Problematically though, Keith had only ever accomplished intimacy with a woman by spying on her; by an invasion of her sovereignty, while relinquishing none of his own.

The news story he'd seen about Ida had been stumbled upon while he was searching the internet for stories on crime. Keith would have gone past the short article about a bank robbery after reading it because the suspects' names rang no bells, but there was a photo. He recognized one of the people in the picture of two women in the back of a police car. Keith had stared at the photo, enlarged it and squinted, his pulse quickening as it came to him. "Fuck!" he'd whispered, realizing he hadn't known Ida at all. Not even her surname.

The focus of the story, and maybe the only reason it made the news at all, was the peculiarity of there being two lady bank robbers. The tone was salacious, implying the women were lovers; a take-off on the Bonnie and Clyde angle.

This idea of Ida as both criminal celebrity and sex object was overwhelmingly arousing for Keith. He needed to be here at her apartment, satisfying a need for some tactile experience. Every object in her apartment now beckoned as a possible fetish object; as an artefact suddenly worthy of notice.

He scrutinized Ida's bookshelf for the first time, for clues to a human personality. The DVDs and the handful of books were all travel related. Keith shook his head. No wonder the woman had been caught; she knew nothing about crime. She should have confided in him. Why hadn't she?

The bedroom. A bedside table drew his attention, the lure

140

of intimacy. One by one he removed the contents. A bottle of Advil, a book, some sort of diary, save that for later, a...

The faint sound of men's voices in the hall outside the apartment, just meaningless background noise, suddenly grew louder, like a volume dial being turned up.

Now, clearly, the men were entering the apartment.

"Ida? Ida? Hello? Ida? one voice called, accompanied by banging on the open door.

"Maybe she's not home." A fainter voice demurred timidly.

"No," said the first guy, obviously older. "She wouldn't leave her door unlocked. Ida!" The tone was aggressive: the sort usually reserved for naughty children. "Where are you? I know you're here."

Keith looked wildly around. He had a right to be here, to some degree, but the voices were threatening because unknown. He stepped into the closet.

The two voices called several more times, one aggressive, one passive. They moved about the apartment. The volume of their voices, to Keith, changed, depending on their proximity to him.

The older of the voices was suddenly coming from inside the bedroom.

"She's not here," said the younger voice from another room.

"No."

"We should leave."

"No. We'll wait. She musta stepped out." The old guy who said this spoke like he was in charge.

"You cool?" asked the young one.

"What's that mean?"

"You calm?"

"Absolutely... You worried? Don't be. Ida's not gonna call the cops and I'm not gonna hurt her. She's gonna give me my share of the money from the bank robbery and then we're gonna walk away."

Keith had begun to perspire and now his stomach felt thin. Hearing a criminal talk about his acts induced nausea the way that swirling on a carnival ride might: dizziness mixed with danger, and delirious pleasure. He'd heard something he shouldn't have.

The two new intruders went silent, now sitting in the living room apparently. The younger one asked if they were still going to the Hayes farm, and received no answer. He said he was against it, and mentioned the virtue of calmness.

Keith started at mention of the name Hayes.

"We should just leave once we get the money," the young voice said.

"I shoulda picked you up later. I'm sorry, really. It's not your worry, what happens. I appreciate the concern but I need to follow this up. People can't kill others with impunity. What kind of world would that be? But this kid they killed was my son. I may not be able to get the one who did the deed but I can take care of Hayes. He's the guy who was behind it, for sure."

"But the cops! That's their job. We get any information you should turn it over, otherwise you become a victim too. I don't care about scum like Hayes but I'm worried about you."

"Fuck!" The older man cut him off. "You're distractin' me. What are we sittin' around for? We came here to find the money. Start lookin'. Tear the place apart if need be. Why don't you start with the kitchen... No wait. I'll do that. Check the bathroom and the hall closet. Look inside every jar or box you find. I'll dig around here and the bedroom."

The word bedroom was the cue for Keith to resume the panic that had ebbed momentarily in fascination and joy at being in the presence of criminality. He needed to get away, the older guy sounded like a killer.

For several minutes, noises came from the living room, not aggressive, nothing smashed, then he heard sounds from the bedroom.

Keith leaned forward, listening, soft noises.

When Louis Henderson swung open the closet door, Keith fell face forward into his arms, like a romantic swoon.

"What the fuck?" Louis blurted, flinging him to the floor.

He looked at the fallen man's hands, no weapon, then stepped forward, pushed some things about that were hanging in the closet, expecting to see Ida.

Keith sat up where he'd landed.

142

"Who the fuck are you?" said Louis. "And where's Ida?"

"I'm her boyfriend and she's in jail," gulped Keith.

"Jail? For what."

"For bank robbery. Her and her lover."

Louis stared at him trying to take it in, then laughed. "Her lover? You gotta be kiddin' me." He sat down on the bed. "God, life can be sweet."

"I just came across it an hour ago," Keith said. They had moved to his apartment so that Louis could see the internet story about Ida and Sally.

Keith was sitting in front of his desk, with Louis occupying a kitchen chair placed at his elbow and reading over Keith's shoulder.

Joseph stood, facing them, his back to the apartment door.

Louis got up, went to the kitchen and began to root around in the cupboards. He found some packing tape, scissors, and binder twine before returning to his chair.

"You're in the clear it looks like," Keith said. "There's no mention of you. It just says 'bout the two women."

Keith had obviously overheard everything that he'd said to Joseph, Louis knew, so he planned to tie him up and cover his mouth in a way that would keep him from calling the cops for a few hours. Enough time that they wouldn't come swooping down on the Hayes farm while he was there. The money from the robbery had been recovered by the cops, that was a done deal, but his business with Hayes was still very much on the agenda.

"How old are you?" Louis asked.

"Twenty-nine."

And Ida is around forty, Louis thought, well done by her.

"I'm plannin' to tie you up," said Louis, "in case you're wonderin'."

"We're not gonna hurt you," Joseph interjected, smiling at the captive.

"No," added Louis. "I got no problems with you, but I want some time to get away."

"You don't need to do that," said Keith. "I won't call the cops."

143

Louis didn't answer.

"I know you're going to tie me up, not so you can get away from here, but because you want to kill Jack Hayes and you want time to get away after."

Joseph paled.

"Clever boy," said Louis. "Not sure why you want to show off your deductive prowess. You might wanna keep in mind that, at the wrong time, with the wrong people, it could get you killed."

"Yes, maybe not my best move," said Keith, "but I want to help."

"Help do what?"

"I know where this Lemony is, the guy the cops are looking for. You musta heard his name, it's been all over the news. He might be the actual killer. You could take him out as well as Hayes."

Louis had been tapping his knee with the scissors but stopped abruptly, inadvertently pointing them in the direction of Keith. His hand bobbed slowly up and down and he appeared ready to speak.

"And I can take you to him," Keith added.

"You say you know where he is?" Louis asked.

"Yes."

"And where's that?"

"At Hayes's farm."

Louis deflated noticeably. "I can find that on my own."

"Not where he's hiding you can't. It's an underground bunker. And I've seen it."

"A bunker?"

"Yes. Not sure, but I think it's a drug lab. They say Hayes is the biggest producer of Ecstasy in the region."

"And you've seen it: the bunker? How's that?" There was a suspicious edge to Louis's question.

"Just nosing around, walking across the field. I knew the place belonged to criminals so I was curious. Maybe it sounds crazy. Anyway, it was dark and the tunnel door was open. I left but I went back a second time and looked inside. I saw this Lemony guy sleeping there."

"God. You sound like there's somethin' missin' in your

brain to not be afraid of people like that. And why would you show me?"

Keith hesitated. "Because it's like you said, they're murderers."

In spite of his faults, like stalking, and his ambitions to be a criminal, Keith also had his moments of moral rectitude. It had already led him to betray the Hayes gang by calling Crime Stoppers when he saw what he thought was a body at the farm. And it was why he'd tried to chop down a school wall when he felt a student was being persecuted. It was also why he liked Louis; seeing him as a primitive rebel or an avenging angel. The guy wasn't about to kill for power; he had good reasons for what he was about to do, which was to enact justice.

Louis set the scissors down on the desk and considered.

"You'll want to go at night," added Keith. "I'm sure they have tons of security. Last time I went, there was someone out looking around, and I think he mighta been after me. But the first night I went, nothing. I was thinking about it. I climbed over the fence in a different spot that first time so maybe it's a place where there's no camera coverage.

Louis stared at Keith, assessing, but appreciating how someone could be enthralled by the idea of danger and crime. "So how'd you meet Ida?" he asked, like he was suddenly speaking to an old friend.

32.

blood soaked the surrounding area

Ted drove down a trail to Little Creek for some speckled trout fishing with his ten-year-old son Kyle. This was their favourite spot along the creek because of the deep pools.

From the crushed grass in the clearing atop the bank, Ted could tell that someone had recently parked and camped there. Whoever it was had left the charred remains of a campfire where they'd also probably pitched a tent.

Climbing out of the car, the pair could hear the rush of water below. They retrieved their fishing kit from the trunk and headed for the path that ran down the embankment.

That's when Ted saw what appeared to be a pair of feet protruding into the clearing at it's far end. At the same time he heard a distinct rustling in the woods beyond.

"Wait Kyle!" he said, reaching out and taking him by the shoulder. "Stop talking."

Kyle went silent, eyes open wide having picked up on his father's alarm.

Ted told his son they were going back to the car while more or less pushing him along with frequent wary glances back at the pair of feet.

Once Kyle was safely ensconced in the vehicle, Ted popped the trunk and pulled out one of his son's aluminium baseball bats.

Edging his way forward, past the car and across the clearing, he called, "Hello? Hello?" as he went. When he was near enough to reach, he extended an arm and used the bat to separate the bushes above the body.

There was a rustle of the underbrush as whatever animal that had been there beat a hasty retreat. It had already had its way with the man's body laying on the ground, and dragged out its entrails. Blood soaked the surrounding area.

Ted scrambled back in horror, threw up, and retreated to his car.

146

33.

wouldn't be the first guy said he was a rock star to get a woman into bed

It was going on for ten PM and Detective Schmidt, working on his final coffee of the day, was determined to finish his report on the death of Lawrence Henderson before going home. He had his hand-written notes in front of him, and was now thoughtfully perusing them. His face was pursed, like he'd eaten a lemon. The notes were too speculative he knew. He would have to make cuts and stick to the facts.

They read:

1. *Lawrence Henderson, was killed on the shore of Little Creek by what appears to have been an axe or hatchet blow to the chest.*

2. *The time of death was very early AM on Friday (note that the ladies in custody for the Carmel Credit Union robbery on Friday, were not in custody at that time).*

3. *The victim has been identified as Lawrence Henderson, similar to the name of Louis Henderson's brother, but different. According to Louis Henderson's family the missing (dead) brother's legal name is/was Larry. No family (or history) has yet been turned up for this particular Lawrence Henderson. It is presumably an alias.*

4. *A search of the victim's premises turned up a purple Capri, reported stolen, and undoubtedly the vehicle used in the credit union robbery.*

5. *No fingerprints were found in the car nor in the house. Everything thoroughly wiped clean.*

6. *The deceased's pickup was located in the city, mid-morning. Residents said it hadn't been parked there long. Fingerprints on it match those on a hatchet found under the front seat, which may be the murder weapon. And the prints don't match those of Lawrence.*

7. *It was surely Louis Henderson who drove the pickup back to the city. The truck received a ticket in the parking lot of a community college. A teacher, who apparently gave the man shelter for the night, told police that the man at first*

appeared to be Louis Henderson but now he's not so sure of it. He said that he'd once seen Louis Henderson perform with his band when they were younger and, although the guy driving the pickup looked like him, he seemed 'pretty dull' whereas the Henderson of twenty years ago was 'a sort of intellectual'. (This decline could be the result of legal and illegal drug use, and of psychiatric intervention.)

8. Louis Henderson is likely still in the city, and armed with the handgun used in the bank robbery.

9. Ida Finger has insisted that a third party was involved in the robbery. This now has credence. She said she'd stayed at Lawrence (Larry) Henderson's house (meaning the women should be viewed as murder suspects in addition to Louis Henderson). The murder was likely part of the armed robbery plan in some way. After the robbery was completed, the intention was possibly that the two women would drive Sally Porter's car back to the city while Louis returned to the Henderson house and switched to the truck. Lawrence could have been killed earlier to get rid of him as a witness and to make sure that he wouldn't object to his truck being taken.

Wilde returned from a fruitless search of Ida Finger's apartment which they'd decided to check after discovering that Louis Henderson was in the city.

Wilde dropped into Schmidt's office, just as Schmidt was finishing up the re-reading of his notes, plopped down and shook his head in the negative. Each frowned at the other as if he was responsible for the recent murder and the complications to their armed robbery case.

"So it looks like there was a man involved after all," said Wilde, "and the guy was Louis Henderson."

"Apparently. My guess is that he went camping with Lawrence, out to the river, and killed him so he could steal his truck. I'm thinking now that Sally Porter was just there for the getaway. She comes up from the city as an accomplice so that the women can drive to Carmel with the money and then switch to Porter's car. So Finger helps Henderson do the credit union then he drops her at the Civic where Sally Porter is waiting. He then goes to Lawrence Henderson's, dumps the purple car and takes his truck. That lets him drive back to the city without fear of getting stopped."

"But why did they need Porter? Finger could have left in the Civic."

"The Civic was stolen so it wasn't a safe car. Porter's, would be far less likely to get flagged on the drive back to the city. If I was a betting man, I'd say that they were also afraid that the farmer who owned the rendezvous spot might stumble across whatever car that was left there so they didn't want to chance leaving Porter's in the cornfield. The Civic was only meant to get the pair back to Carmel where Porter's car was legally parked on a side street. She undoubtedly hiked it out to where the Civic was stashed so she could show Finger where she'd parked."

"What confuses me though is that Louis Henderson had no reason to kill Lawrence Henderson. That makes no sense."

Schmidt made a note. "He did though," he said. "All three did if Lawrence wasn't part of the plan and objected to them using his truck. Plus he was a potential witness. Don't know why Louis took him to the creek to kill him though and not do it at his place."

"Maybe that goes in the women's favour. If all three were complicit in the murder, why not just kill him out back of the house? It could be argued that Louis Henderson took the guy out to the woods so the women wouldn't know what he was up to. He coulda then made up some story about why the guy didn't return with him."

"Fuck," said Schmidt, who didn't like loose ends or possible misreadings.

"And if they knew he was dead, it's not likely that Ida Finger would keep mentioning Larry Henderson as if he was her alibi."

"Well, I'm not so sure about that one. If they knew about the killing, or were involved, then acting innocent about the connection, even pointing to it, would be a way of throwing all the blame on Louis."

"Which seems to be their approach."

"Yeah, so that line of reasoning makes the most sense to me," added Schmidt.

149

"Roll the dice. All or nothing… It's gonna come down to what Louis Henderson says when we find him."

"But you know what I still find hard to make sense of? That we still don't know if Lawrence Henderson is Larry Henderson, Louis's brother. We need to show his picture to Louis's family. Plus, the college professor, the only person, who saw Louis Henderson in the past, thinks that he could be an impostor: someone just saying he's Louis."

"Maybe Louis lied to the women. He wouldn't be the first guy said he was a rock star to get a woman into bed."

"Which would make Lawrence a fraud too. Nothing really makes sense unless the men are the real Henderson brothers or they're both impostors. Maybe they're brothers and knocked off the real Hendersons to steal their identities. Doppelgangers maybe. And maybe the old lady that Ida Finger mentioned – and said Louis called her his grandmother – may really have been the phoney Lawrence's mother. It's a mess."

At that moment a constable stuck his head through the door and said, "Knock, knock."

"Yeah?" Schmidt asked.

"Just got this sir," and he proffered a piece of paper. "Foreign Affairs says that Larry Henderson definitely committed suicide in Uruguay. They're positive."

34.

Sunday: longing for the golden age of gangsterdom

It was slightly past midnight. Keith and Louis were slouched on the sofa in the living room of Keith's apartment with Louis fielding questions and loving the attention merited by being someone in the know on criminality.

Joseph sat quietly at the window, listening and watching vigilantly, and becoming increasingly alarmed at just how much Louis was revealing. Keith was now privy to a truckload of personal, criminal information.

Joseph had been nervous since, when sneaking a look out the window earlier, he'd spotted a cop car pulling up to the front entrance of the apartment building. He'd advised Louis and Keith of it but neither felt threatened enough to let it interrupt their confab.

Keith had taken his cue from Louis, and Louis had correctly surmised that the nature of the police visit was to check on Ida's place to see if he was there.

Seeing no harm in answering Keith's questions about the bank robbery – since they were about to engage in a joint criminal endeavour – Louis described it in minute detail, even explaining the plan he'd worked up with Ida in the event they were caught; to say that she'd been compelled to participate.

Keith was earnestly fascinated at this insight into a crime, a subject he thought he knew well, but only from a distance. "Think she's telling the cops that line?"

"She better be. It's her only chance of gettin' off."

The subject shifted to guns, at one point, with Louis even showing Keith his handgun. Desperately wanting to touch it, Keith stroked it sensually while listening and longing for the golden age of gangsterdom when it had been bought by Louis at Dutchie's on Front Street. He knew that story by now too.

"Guess it got you through a lot, eh?" said Keith.

Louis chuckled, at the memories presumably, of the good times between him and his gun, with a wistfulness that suggested he might be carrying baby pictures of it in his wallet.

Eventually, the conversation came back around to Ida.

Louis felt guilty, he said. Because of his great scheme to knock over a bank, Ida was now in jail. "Never in a million years would she have done something like this on her own. I gave her a chance to be greedy and she took it. Forget the betrayal to me, I had it comin' probably, but now I owe her somethin'…" and, after apparently considering the matter, added, "I'd get her out of jail if I could." Ida, the real Ida, was suddenly becoming visible to him.

And Keith, now the attentive boyfriend, was keen for a jailbreak.

That's impossible, he was told, to his disappointment.

"I only meant that I'd like to pay her bail but I have no money," Louis said.

Keith countered with the idea of Louis sending the prosecutor some sort of written confession. "You could get a sworn affidavit from a lawyer and take the blame. As long as you don't get caught you'll be good to go."

Louis perked up at the thought. "You know, that's not half bad," he said slowly, considering the idea. He was going to be on the run anyway, and with several already procured IDs available to him he could become someone else. Louis Henderson was a disposable identity. It wouldn't matter who was looking for him as he was about to fall off the map of the world.

"Let's do it!" Louis said abruptly. "Only I don't want no lawyer involved cus I wanna do it now."

They penned the confession together, then Louis signed it, and Joseph and Keith were witnesses. The latter folded it up and put it into his back pocket, literally and figuratively, to be presented to the police in a few days, after Louis was out of the country.

To Lemony's way of thinking, post-modern literature could not have occurred without film and advertising. The ambiguity of the visual and the awareness of its false reality.

He was laying on a blanket, on the floor of the empty lab, having found it too constricting and hot in the hay loft. He continued his contemplation of imagery and resolved to tell his publisher he was no longer interested in doing a book on how to find a literary agent. He wanted to get a long way away and work on something else. Haiku. Loaded images. With the cops after him and his interests beckoning, it was time to go.

It wasn't just literary considerations that were prompting his decision. The evening before his first trip to the farm, a few weeks earlier, he'd been semi-drunk and lolling in the garden of his editor and the guy's wife, at a party, when he overheard them talking. They were savaging a poet who he knew and considered to be a friend. Their comments on Khmer verse were ridiculous in the extreme, he thought, to the point of offensiveness. Who would want to be associated with such philistines?

A noise on the ladder from the barn suddenly intruded itself into his consciousness.

The light was off so the figure he soon saw was just a silhouette against the faint light coming from the barn above. Lemony watched the shape painfully making its way downwards. From the awkwardness, he knew it was Jack Hayes. Lemony's initial impulse was to call out Jack's name but he stopped himself for reasons he wasn't consciously aware of. Instead, he just lay still and observed.

Keith and Louis trudged along the side of County Road 18 through the two AM darkness on their way to pay their social visit on Jack Hayes.

Back at the apartment building was a stolen white two-door Civic – which Joseph had pronounced 'pretty sweet' – that Louis had grabbed after dumping Larry's pickup near the psych hospital. It had been decided, by Louis, that it was best to leave the Civic in the visitor's parking rather than have it announce their presence at the Hayes farm by leaving it on the side of the road. Better to hike over and keep their visit a nice surprise.

"Why did she dump you, if you don't mind me asking?" Keith said, the current conversation being about Stone Cutter and his mother.

"Naw, I don't mind," said Louis, always ready to ad lib

about his past, tailoring it to his audience, creating a fictional version of himself to hide behind and remain invisible. He never remembered previous versions. "It was cus I admitted to an infidelity; a stupid thing to do. Two of them I guess you could say. Guess I had a momentary crisis of conscience. My wife was a party girl who couldn't care less about bein' a mother and was bangin' everyone she could, but I was the dummy who confessed. She got sole access to our son cus of who her daddy is, and cus I got painted as a druggie and burned out rocker. Kinda redundant maybe."

"What was…"

"And I…sorry," said Louis. "What were you gonna say?"

"This place she was living in sounds pretty amazing."

"Yeah, it was. Her old man is Dr. Cutter, the famous heart surgeon." Louis paused, but receiving no confirmation of recognition, continued. "He's like the richest guy in the world and way over-protective of Daddy's little girl. I couldn't have cared less that my wife liked to go out partying 'cept she would take Stone with her. I tried to keep track of their whereabouts so I could keep an eye on him. The last night I saw Stone, I was hanging around the entrance gates when this guy named Sean leaves. He knew who I was and didn't seem to hate me so I asked him about my son. Oh, I should mention that this Sean guy is creepy, like pedophile creepy, although I guess, lookin' back, he probably wasn't one. Anyway, doesn't matter. He said how he'd been babysittin' and it was the best day of his life. And I was thinkin', like what the fuck does that mean, you know? Babysittin' is the best moment of your life? And just then, Daisy – that's the wife – comes home, and she's got my daughter with her."

"Your daughter?"

"Yeah. She's older than the boy. Different mother. That's another story. So I got beside the car window and tried to talk to Daisy. The gate came up and she gunned the car into the compound. I was gonna follow but the gates shut and two security guards grabbed me to stop me gettin' in. My daughter jumped out of the car and opened the door in the wall beside the gate but they pushed her back inside the compound after throwing me on the ground. They slammed the door in my face and locked it. I yelled and screamed and kicked the door awhile. Anyway, after a lot of effort, I eventually found a way and got inside the estate. At the party I saw Daisy's old man…"

"Jesus! It's here."

"You sure, Stone? This is the exact spot?"

"Positive." Keith ignored being called the wrong name because it thrilled him.

"Yeah."

Keith had rightly guessed that the point of entry he'd used on his first visit, when no one had come looking for him, was a blind spot for the farm's cameras. He and Louis were retracing that first route exactly.

"Okay," said Louis. "Time we shut up. Lead on to the tunnel."

As an enthused Keith began to scale the fence, Louis grabbed his arm. "And go slow. I'm an old man."

Jack paused at the bottom of the ladder waiting for the pain from his burned arm to subside. He soon turned, dug out his flashlight, and switched it on. The overhead light would be visible up in the barn, and probably even in the enclosed loft due to slim gaps between the floorboards, so better to not use it. Discovery of his presence would raise questions about why he was in the bunker. There was only Lemony left upstairs, but even one person was enough to worry about.

Jack unzipped the jacket he'd worn for the occasion, and reached for the bundle of money he'd been given the day before. It was again tucked inside his shirt. He tossed it onto the table.

He knelt, cursed his arm pain again, and took out a screwdriver from his jacket pocket. He used it to unscrew a square metal plate in the floor of perhaps sixty by sixty centimetres.

With the hand attached to his good arm, Jack reached through the hole in the centre of the plate, picked it up, and placed it off to one side. Leaning over, he input the combination and opened the door to a small safe.

It was only as he raised himself up to reach for the money

on the table that the beam of light from his flashlight played across Lemony, laying on the floor on the other side of the table, wide-awake and watching.

Jack jumped to his feet, reached back behind the ladder and flicked on the overhead light.

"Fuck Fabio!" he started. "You scared the shit outta me! What are you doing here?"

"I couldn't sleep because of the heat up in the hayloft."

"You're not supposed to be in the lab at night," Jack said, his voice reflecting controlled fury (although there was no such rule).

"Sorry. I didn't know."

"Yeah, well you shoulda. There's somethin' strange about you being here." Jack's restraint was quickly dissipating. "Whata you playin' at?" He reached into his coat and touched the handle of the handgun tucked inside the shoulder holster he'd taken to wearing after the murder of Al Jackson.

"Whoa! Whoa! Calm down." Lemony got to his knees, aware of the danger. "I don't see what there is to be so angry about. I won't do it again." He slowly climbed to his feet, eyes on Jack.

"You shouldn't have done it this time."

Immediately after reaching the floor of the tunnel, Louis and Keith saw the light from the flashlight in the lab, its beam darting up and down the wall where the tunnel turned. Pausing, they listened for a moment to two voices.

"Shh," Louis whispered in Keith's ear, adding, "No flashlight." He took Keith's arm and moved forward.

Keith felt emboldened by the lead of someone he emulated.

Louis's handgun was in a jacket pocket, wrapped in a plastic bag in case of rain. He removed it and dropped the bag onto the floor. He stuck his nose around the turn in the tunnel. Never one to not grasp the drama of a situation, he choose the moment Jack said, "You shouldn't have done it this time," to step into view.

"Neither of you should have done it," Louis said, pointing his handgun at them.

156

Both men turned, started at sight of the gun, and immediately stopped talking, a frozen tableaux of incomprehension.

Keith stepped out from behind Louis, adding even more confusion.

"Fuck, Fabio. I see you brought your boys with you," Jack said.

"Don't look at me asshole," replied Lemony, their shared situation eliminating the deferential tone he always employed with his boss, now equals in humiliation. "I don't know what this is."

"It's about the money obviously. You and your biker buddies here…"

"No," said Louis. "It's about the kid you killed."

Lemony was loud and insistent. "I never killed anyone in my life, or even came close to it?"

"I've never killed anyone either," Jack said slowly, his eyes locked on Louis.

"You're a liar Jack," interjected Keith. "You killed Al Jackson just last week. Why don't you tell us what happened to Stone Cutter?"

"Who?" Jack was obviously taken aback by this odd, rodent-like man. "And who the fuck are you?" Looking back at Louis he added, "I know you, I think."

"Then why kill my son? Was it drug money he owed you? Or what?"

"Your son? I swear to you, I don't know who you're talkin' about."

"He means the dead kid on the news," Lemony said. "The media were giving out my name about his murder, but I had nothing to do with it. It had to be you Jack; you're a sadistic prick. I remember that day last week when you said you had a couple of problem people to take care of. I can guess which two you were talking about."

Sensing a lull, a glimmer of vulnerability in Louis's demeanour, Jack grabbed for his gun. Jerked it from its shoulder holster. And swung it out in front of him.

Louis and Jack fired simultaneously. The deafening reverberations from the shots echoed through the bunker.

Jack fell, a hole in his chest.

Keith spun from a bullet to the shoulder. Dropped to his knees.

Louis looked down at Jack. Then back at Lemony. No threat. He sensed, rather than saw, Keith begin to pitch to his side. He reached out, caught hold of a sleeve, and slowly lowered his partner to the cool concrete floor.

Lemony's eyes had stayed on Louis. A gun barrel demands attention. But when it swung away, as Keith went over, Lemony stabbed out his arm, snatching up the bundle of money on the table.

He hit the overhead light switch as he took his first step on the ladder. Then rushed furiously upwards through the darkness.

Louis glanced back over his shoulder, took a wild shot in Lemony's general direction, but missed.

Unfazed, he went back to tending Keith. He wasn't certain that Lemony knew anything about his son Stone's murder. On the other hand, Jack Hayes definitely did, and he was dead. He was the target. His denials weren't worth a thing.

Louis told Keith to lay still, arose, found the light switch, clicked it on, then checked on Jack. The proverbial doornail.

That's when he saw the stacks of money inside the open safe in the floor.

Louis hesitated. Jack likely had armed security on the way, rushing from the house, but the money demanded action. He ran back up the tunnel to retrieve the plastic bag he'd discarded earlier, and rapidly filled it with the money. He closed the safe, and put the plate in place. Still hearing nothing from above, he hand-tightened the screws that he'd spotted laying beside Jack on the floor. Best if the cops don't know about the safe. He then stuffed the bag inside his shirt.

Keith was oblivious to these proceedings, absorbed with his own troubles. But he now began climbing to his knees.

"C'mon man," Louis said. "Time to get up." He slipped a hand under Keith's armpit and helped him stand. They staggered their way along the tunnel.

"I can't make it up the ladder," Keith gasped. "I'm too weak. I'm losing a lot of blood."

"We'll get you home..."

"No. I can't make it home, I need an ambulance."

"Well let's get out and I'll call one. Someone will have heard the shots. Trust me, we gotta go."

With Louis behind him, shoulder propped under his partner's butt, Keith got to the top of the ladder before flopping onto the ground.

"Gimme your phone," said Louis attempting to dig into Keith's back pant pocket.

"No, you go. I'll call." Keith spoke is a raspy whisper, knocking Louis's hand away. "No point turning yourself in. You need to go."

Louis considered. "Let's get you under cover by the outer fence first, before Jack's security gets here." They could hear a dog barking madly, and it was closing in on them.

Keith, allowing himself to be supported, got over the barbed wire fence, and across the field. Both men were drenched in sweat by the time Keith made it over the second fence to be positioned upright in the ditch, hidden in the impenetrable two AM darkness. "Leave me your gun in case they come," he whispered.

"Naw. Then the cops'll think you shot Hayes."

"Good, let em, I'll say it was self-defence."

Louis sighed loudly in frustration. He didn't like the idea of someone taking the blame for him, but then again Keith might need the gun; Hayes's security people or the dog could show up at any second. And pissing around arguing wouldn't help; Keith needed an ambulance.

"Okay, phone Emergency then," said Louis.

Laboriously, his partner pressed keys on the phone. "Yeah, 9-1-1?" Keith began, growling. "I killed the bastard cus he drew on me. His worst mistake ever."

Fuck, Louis thought, this asshole wants to go to jail. He waited until the call was done before handing Keith his gun and then sprinting off up the road.

"I'll leave you some money," he yelled back but the words were lost in the wind and Keith didn't hear. In any case, since he knew nothing of the money, the remark would have made no sense to him.

159

35.

if you wanna meet randy women, go to a reactionary church

"There's almost three-hundred grand here!" Louis said, as he pushed his chair back from the kitchen table.

"Fuck," Joseph said, eyebrows raised.

"Fuck indeed."

The two men looked anxiously at each other. The elation they'd shared, twenty minutes before when Louis had upended his plastic bag and strewn bills across the table, now gave way to wariness.

"They're going to be looking for us," Joseph said, vigorously nodding his head.

"They're already lookin' for us... I mean, lookin' for me." Louis eyed Joseph. "You don't have to come with me, you know. I can take you home. It's dull there, but it's safe."

"No, I want to go. I don't like killing but I know you had no choice. I still want to go."

"For this amount of money, some people'll never give up lookin' for me," Louis said, "and if you're with me, you'll be in danger too."

"People have been chasing you forever, and I've been around you enough to get used to it."

"Okay then." The question was put to rest.

"What're you going to do with it?" Joseph asked soberly.

Louis only made something like an exasperated whoosh sound.

"You should buy your camper," Joseph said, brightening. "Head for Saratoga. Live your dream."

"I was livin' it before, I don't think dreams should be tainted by money, like the capitalists' American dream, but you're right; now we can go in style. The money is ours."

"Then you can give some money to charity. My mother always said that a real man looks after the weak."

"Well no disrespect to your mother but that sort of attitude's not gonna get you laid. It's the phony manliness you don that does the trick. If you wanna meet randy women, go

160

to a reactionary church and talk about how awful and weak poor people are."

"I didn't mean it to attract women, but just to do something nice."

"Alright then." Louis leaned back in his chair and thought the matter over. "Okay," he said eventually, "how 'bout we say one hundred grand for us to get the camper and set ourselves up. And we gotta leave Keith his share, so a hundred grand for him, same as us."

"But..."

"Which reminds me." Louis jumped up, turned on the TV, found a local news station and set the sound low. "I wanna hear what's happenin'," he explained.

The two stared at the screen and waited fruitlessly.

Louis eventually glanced at Joseph and said, "We could leave the last hundred thousand for Ida. Let her take those vacations she wants and maybe start a business. She has some screwy idea about making greeting cards with Sally."

Joseph looked uncertain.

"That's almost like charity," added Louis, "helping unemployed people. Plus they're gonna have some lawyer's expenses unless they figure out 'bout Legal Aid. We're all on the same team aren't we: you, me, Keith, Sally, Larry, and Ida? And nothing teaches teamwork like committing a capital offence. It's all about connectivity."

"Okay, I like that," said Joseph.

They were about to leave, despite being exhausted from lack of sleep. "We gotta get outa the country as soon as possible," Louis had explained. "You never know what Keith's gonna say to the cops and if my name gets mentioned then my picture'll be all over the news."

Keith and Ida's portions of the money were stacked on Ida's kitchen table with a note of explanation. Louis and Joseph had come down to Ida's apartment for safety. At any moment the cops were sure to be all over Keith's place.

A TV news story caught Joseph's attention. A Conservative politician was engaging in some Orwellian doublethink about less environmental protections being more. Joseph exploded

161

with laughter. He took a childish delight in fairy stories.

Louis leaned towards the TV after the next news story had begun.

"Details are uncertain," said an on-site reporter, standing at the side of County Road 18 with the Hayes barn in the distant background. "All we're being told at the moment, by a police spokesman, is that Jack Hayes is dead. That he was shot on his farm during the night and that a man has been taken into custody. Police are being tight-lipped but there is speculation that this could be gang and drug related, perhaps retaliation for the killing of Al Jackson several days ago by Jack Hayes. Police said at the time that the killing was self-defence."

"So if Keith's in custody he must be okay," said Joseph, relieved.

"Well, maybe not okay, but he's alive. That's good. What I wanted to know."

The pair continued to watch until the story concluded.

"Well, we're off," said Louis slapping his knees and standing up. He had taken a single step in the direction of the screen when his brother's picture flashed up.

"That's…" began Joseph.

"Shh, shh," Louis waived at him to be silent.

The two listened to a very brief story from the north of the province about a man named Lawrence Henderson who'd been killed with a hatchet. "Police are looking for his brother, Louis Henderson, famous as the singer of the band God's Gift to Women which disbanded years ago. He is not listed as a suspect but may have information that can shed light on events." A photo of a much younger looking Louis flashed up on the screen.

"Jesus!" said Louis, "a hatchet. Who the fuck…" his voice trailed off, remembering the hatchet on the floor of Larry's truck.

"Why are the cops looking for you?" asked Joseph. "Poor Larry! This is terrible. Louis?"

"Wait, wait," Louis said. "I need to think." He went to the window and stared outside.

Joseph fidgeted, watching his friend's back, until Louis

162

returned to the couch and sat down.

"I told Ida I thought Larry was involved in something illegal," Louis began, clearly speaking to himself, sorting things through. "It musta caught up to him. Ida's probably told the cops that we stayed at his house and now they wanna talk to me. I don't have anything to say to them and if I go up north to find who did this I'll end up in jail for the robbery. I think the best thing to do is to head for the States like we planned. Give some time for the cops to sort it out. If they don't, I'll come back up in the fall and see what I can find out... Jesus."

"Sorry about your brother."

Louis looked at Joseph as if he didn't understand the statement or had simply forgotten the presence of someone else in the room. "What? Oh yeah. Well he died before. He's the sort who goes on livin'. Anyway, I did my mourning for him already. What we gotta do is head south, now. Hopefully we can get across the border with you drivin' and me in the trunk. You got your ID and license?"

"Always," Joseph said proudly.

"Good. You're a good driver." An intentionally gratuitous statement from the new Louis that caused Joseph to beam. "We'll take the car, and once we're across the border we'll buy the camper. I mean, after we get some of our money converted to American dollars."

As they drove, Joseph said, "So we're gonna have to change our names?"

"I'm debatin' about you. I already have multiple IDs. We'll get you one too; a U.S. ID."

"With a new name?"

"Not necessarily, but that's an interesting field of study." Louis hesitated. The last time he'd trotted out this pony to do a few laps he'd been called an 'ignorant knucklehead' by some guy he'd been running with, but he had more faith in Joseph. "There are two ways to hide, and I've thought about this over the years. One way is to change your name and create a whole new identity. That's one school of thought or, I guess, really, one option. There's another way too. I got this

163

one from a friend of mine who knew a guy. What that guy would do was just change his address. He was a writer, did books on handicapping. His name was WJ Brown That was his legal name, just the initials; had it changed when he was young. All of his writing was under the name of WJ Brown. Everyone knew him as WJ. He'd move when things heated up and would choose a new name that fit the initials: like Wendell Jason Brown, or Wallace James Brown, names along those lines, you understand. Always a W and a J. He would be listed as the longer name in anything official but he'd tell the locals to call him WJ. So even though he kept the same name with people he conversed with, no one could find him through official sources cus he was listed under the two new Christian names rather than WJ. It's called hiding in plain sight. I think he kept his old social insurance number and filed his taxes using a phoney address. No one coulda found him cus of that though. The government keeps these things private."

"So no one ever found him?"

"Not as far as I know."

"How did he get his publisher's pay cheques? Because I think if he told them where he lived, so they'd come in the mail, someone could trace him."

"I don't know. Direct deposit I guess."

Joseph looked satisfied. It wasn't because he was an idiot that he couldn't appreciate idiocy but because he knew so little of the world.

36.

know anything about a cap belonging to Stonewall Cutter?

It was early in the evening before his doctor cleared Keith to be interviewed by the police. Twelve hours of sleep and a blood transfusion had done wonders. The medication would slow him down but he was capable of holding a conversation.

Detective Swain, notepad in hand, stood at the foot of the bed "Did you go to the farm to shoot Hayes?" he asked.

"Not at all. I went lookin' for this Lemony guy I'd been hearin' about cus it said on the radio he killed my friend Stone Cutter." Keith's voice was taking on the intonations of Louis Henderson's voice. "Lemony wasn't there but Hayes was. I confronted him. Demanded to know where Lemony was. Bastard pulled a gun and shot me, so I pulled mine and ended him. Self-defence."

"Stone Cutter was your friend?"

"Yeah."

"Your fingerprints are all over Cutter's apartment."

"Like I said, we were friends."

"What do you know about his involvement with Hayes?"

"Nothin'. I suppose he was pushing drugs for him and ripped him off so Hayes sent Lemony after him. Nothin' to do with me."

Swain scribbled. "Did you have any involvement with Hayes yourself?"

"Naw."

"What about Al Jackson?"

"Naw."

"Ever been to the Hayes farm before?"

They suspect, thought Keith, that I made the call reporting a body. Not that it mattered; he'd planned to mention it. "I went there a few days ago. Saw a body and reported it to Crime Stoppers."

"You didn't put the body there."

"I didn't."

"Know anything about a ball cap belonging to Stonewall

Cutter: black with a trucking company logo on the front?"

"Yeah, he gave it to me. I lost it at the farm that first night. I ran when I saw the body. Right into a tree. Cap went flying."

"Why did you go to the farm before you heard anything on the media about Leonard Boissoneault?"

"Suspicious. Heard someone in our building say they thought Stone was involved with Hayes and the bikers who hang out at his farm. Went to nose around. It was after I knew who killed Stone that I went back the second time to find the guy."

A long silence followed while Swain thought. It hit him all at once, the realization that he had absolutely no evidence to support the idea of Hayes having any involvement in the murder of Stonewall Cutter. No real reason to even assume it was a murder. It had just been that stupid ball cap. For all he knew, Keith had planted the cap to throw suspicion on Hayes. Fuck, fuck, fuck, he thought. "He…" Swain said. He wanted to resume his questioning but was sidetracked by the thoughts elbowing their way into his head. Fuck, he was going to look silly. He hated this sonofabitch on the bed who talked like he was hip to something or other. "Let's return to the first visit and the body you say you saw, the body you quite possibly put there…"

"Can I sleep?" Keith cut him off, appearing to swoon, to great theatrical effect. "I'm exhausted."

A nurse stepped forward and signalled to Swain who sighed and angrily flipped closed his notepad. He was going to nail this bastard.

37.

Monday: Chartrand's on about Moaris

"He had three sons," old man Chartrand was telling Constable Bradshaw at the front desk. "Bruce, John and Sheldon." Chartrand was a lonely local retiree who often made his way to the station to shoot the breeze with the boys. When not trudging up the shoulder of the highway or leaning on fences to chat up farmers, this was where he came.

"Wasn't there a sister?"

"Yeah. Can't remember her name. Nice looking girl. Sheldon went to New Zealand. Got married. Had three kids. Damn nice guy. Upbeat. Optimistic. I chummed with him at school. Married a Maori." He leaned his head forward. "Not that I have anything against them. They've had to deal with a lot of prejudice I'm sure."

Constable Bill Phelps standing in the detachment's kitchen, was eavesdropping while rinsing out his coffee cup. Chartrand, he knew, didn't hate Maoris only because he'd never met one. If he had, his hate would have been up front, same as it was with every other race not his own. The old man especially loathed Italians, and sounded as if he would condone killing Germans and Japanese on sight. He was still fighting WWII.

Phelps picked up his hat, shouted out to Bradshaw that he was going on patrol and left by the back door. On the steps he passed another officer, a long-timer like himself, named David Went.

"Careful, Chartrand's on about Moaris," Phelps said.

Went smiled, then, as if remembering something, pivoted on the top step and called, "Bill wait! I wanna talk to you for a second."

Phelps turned and looked up.

"There's somethin' I need to talk to you about." Went glanced left and right. Only farms in sight. He walked down the steps.

Phelps watched quizzically.

"I was workin' on the weekend," Went said in a

conspiratorial half whisper, "you know, on that axe murder case up on the creek; asking about for that detective." He turned his head left and right, again ensuring they were alone. "What's his name? You know, the one who was here for the bank robbers."

"Wilde?"

"No, the other guy."

"Schmidt."

"Right. The German fella. Anyway, he had me askin' round, talkin' to locals, you know, cus they'll talk to me cus I'm one of them. A few of them were sayin' that Lawrence Henderson was bringin' up smokes from the reserve on the border, selling them through the variety store in town. Guy at the store denied it, but whatta you expect. Anyway, one of the kids at the high school says Henderson had a partner." He paused.

"Okay." Phelps had a premonition of what was coming; felt the adrenalin surging. "And who was that?"

"Don't know. Guy couldn't say. I wouldn't have bothered with it cus Henderson's dead and I figure we know who killed him, so who cares 'bout his sellin' smokes, but Schmidt told me to keep askin' round. He didn't say why."

"Maybe he's not convinced about who killed Henderson." Phelps frowned at everything, at standing here waiting patiently for something he didn't want to hear, at a detective who kept on investigating even after a case was done, at this fucking job in general.

"I suppose. Or confirming his case. Anyway, there's somethin' I gotta tell you Bill. I was comin' home on Friday morning, and I saw a pickup in the field behind your place. It was parked beside that old log building at the edge of the bush. You know..."

"And?"

"And the door to the shed was wide open."

The 'outside bedroom', Phelps mentally corrected him. The shed was behind the house.

"It was a dark green Mazda," Went continued, "same as Henderson's. Didn't think anything of it; figured your boy had one of his buddies over. It wasn't till after we found

168

Henderson's body and started lookin' for a green Mazda that I remembered what I saw."

And the shed, thought Phelps, is where Reg keeps his hatchet. He felt a surging anger and he wanted to take it out on Went.

"Look, I'm not sayin' anything," said Went. "And I won't, 'less you tell me to – we gotta look out for each other – and I won't even ask around about Henderson's partner 'less you want me to. Your boy's a good kid. No reason to get into anything he did in the past. Not like he was involved in what happened to the crazy guy."

"I want you to investigate, if that's what your supposed to do. Don't know why you wouldn't. That's your job," said Phelps with restrained bitterness.

Went hesitated. Suggesting that Henderson's partner in crime was Bill's son was bad enough, but in this case it also meant throwing it out that his kid might be involved in an unsolved murder. "Yeah, yeah, course I will. But I won't report the truck I saw at your place for now. Maybe you should talk to your boy."

"I'll do that." Softening noticeably, Phelps added, "Thanks Davie."

Constable Phelps drove straight home, then across the grassy field behind it, dodging scrub and rocks. At the furthest perimeter of the field he pulled his car up in front of a cabin, the other three sides of which were surrounded by bush. It would be strange if Reg was in fact using it, Phelps thought, since the kid was always deathly afraid of being in it. Triggered terrifying memories apparently. The fucking thing should have been torn down years ago! Phelps was now angry at himself, as if demolishing the building would have prevented this whole damn thing.

The door handle was stiff, rusty, and not locked. He swung the door open. Phelps didn't need to give himself time for his eyes to adjust to the dim light to see the full green garbage bags piled on the floor. In spite of knowing not to touch them he prodded one with the back of his hand and felt the shape of a cigarette carton.

169

After exiting, Bill went to the shed. No hatchet.

Reg was still asleep in bed when his father found him.

"Reg! Reg," Phelps said, shaking him. The light snoring stopped. "Get up. I gotta talk to you about the bags of smokes in the outside bedroom."

Reg, on his back, opened his eyes wide and said nothing.

"And I want to know why Lawrence Henderson's truck was here on Friday morning...after he was killed."

Reg put a hand over his face.

Bill straightened up and kicked the bed frame. "Get the fuck outta bed!" he yelled.

"I'm sorry, Dad," Reg began to cry. "It was an accident."

"I know it was." Bill's voice became gentler. "I know you. It'll be okay." And he meant it. The kid needed his support.

38.

Tuesday: he wanted to nail this vermin

Keith looked at the photo of himself on the front page of the local paper, and felt as viscerally excited as a Chihuahua humping a leg. The headline read: *IS THIS THE FACE OF A GOOD GANGSTER?*

It was like his buddy Louis had said: 'make your dreams materialize'.

The journalist had written that Keith Shadwell, charged in the murder of known gangster Jack Hayes, had gone to the Hayes farm to confront him about that one's suspected involvement in the killing of Stonewall Cutter, who was a friend of Shadwell's. These facts, according to the journalist, had come from a 'reliable police source' who'd also said that Shadwell was claiming self-defence. Furthermore, the source alleged that some police brass saw Shadwell as a hero for taking out a killer who'd destroyed many lives, and for exposing a major drug lab at the same time.

From Keith's perspective, it couldn't have been scripted any better.

For Detective Swain, again standing by Keith's bed, it was supremely annoying. He wanted to nail this vermin – this fucker who'd humiliated him – but there was just no support for it: public or professional. The papers and his superiors loved the psycho in front of him!

Swain's line of attack was that people who aren't involved in the rackets don't usually walk around with guns and visit the drug labs of gangsters in the middle of the night. "So where'd you get the gun?" he asked Keith.

"I got it from a guy named Louis Henderson. You can check the serial number. He bought it from Dutchie's on Front 'bout thirty years ago."

Swain noted it. "And why did he give it to you?"

"He didn't. I took it from his glove compartment for my own protection."

"When you went to the farm to confront Hayes."

Keith looked over at his lawyer, Kale Armor, standing off

171

to the side, who slowly gave a single bob of his head. "No, it was when I went to the farm to see if I could find that Lemony guy and make a citizen's arrest. That was my goal; justice meted out by the courts. I didn't expect to run into Hayes. I'm no vigilante."

"So who's this Henderson guy and how did you meet him?"

"Louis Henderson. He's Stone Cutter's father. He dropped in on me after he'd heard about his son's death. He knew we were best friends."

"Not something that would happen if there was any suspicion that my client was involved in his son's murder," threw in Armor.

Swain tuned him out. "No one's saying that…yet. So where do we get hold of this Henderson?"

"You won't," said Keith.

"Met some sort of bad end did he?" said Swain.

"Not at all. He's on the lam and laying low."

His lawyer visibly winced at the TV drama lingo.

"Look in the cupboard. In the back pocket of my jeans. There's a confession that Henderson asked me to turn over to the police. Looks to me like the cops up north screwed up."

Swain winced. God he hated this smug little prick. And he cursed the weather gods. By the time they'd picked up Shadwell, near the Hayes farm, a torrential rain was falling. It had obliterated all the footprints in the vicinity of the lab entrance; footprints that might have confirmed whether or not Shadwell had gone there by himself.

As Swain dug in the cupboard for the note, Kale Armor smiled at Keith. It was the lawyer's view that Keith might get off altogether and his client had said nothing that would undermine his defence. Quite the contrary actually.

39.

perplexed and unhappy police detectives

By nine that evening the litany of things the two perplexed and unhappy police detectives were upset about had increased.

Provincial Detectives Wilde and Schmidt were preparing an update.

"So do we believe this note was signed by the real Louis Henderson?" asked Wilde, twisting a pencil wedged between his fingers.

"We have to. It checked out that Henderson is Stonewall Cutter's father."

"That doesn't make the person claiming to be Louis Henderson, the real Louis Henderson."

"No, but we really have no reason to doubt who he is. The gun used in the Hayes shooting belonged to the actual Louis Henderson, according to Dutchie's records. The fingerprints on it match those on the confession and inn the stolen Mazda pick-up. Seems conclusive. It was only us doubting this guy was Louis Henderson. City police haven't mentioned any confusion. We say anything publicly, we'll look like conspiracy theorists. The only real uncertainty is whether this guy who was murdered – Lawrence – is Louis's brother. Louis's family refuses to look at the body and insist their son died in Uruguay in an apparent suicide. They told me that even if the corpse was Larry, come home, that since he hadn't called them, and had gone into hiding, that they want nothing to do with him."

Wilde smirked. "Into hiding? Who'd be dumb enough to go into hiding simply by changing their first name, but keeping the same initial?"

"Makes for an interesting conundrum."

"How so?"

"How do you prosecute anyone for killing a person who the government insists is already dead?" He laughed and turned on his computer.

"Both women are out now?" Wilde interjected.

"Yeah. Porter left with her old man yesterday and this afternoon came back and bailed out Finger."

"And we're going to accept Henderson's confession?"

"I suppose so. I'm leaning towards believing the women."

"Really?" Wilde was surprised at the change of heart.

"Sure. Porter parked her car in Carmel and walked a kilometre to where the bank robbers switched cars. Her car's still there. We know that's where the women were heading and they don't deny they were planning to use Porter's car for their getaway. But that doesn't contradict the possibility that they meant to leave the stolen money in Carmel."

"But the knife we found in the field; that's a weapon that she admits to using against someone."

"Right, but she used it, if we believe the women, to free Finger from a kidnapper. Finding the knife only helps her case. It wasn't for the robbery or for protection later, so it must have been to rescue her friend. I don't think we want to pursue charges there."

"So, do the charges of armed robbery against Finger get dropped?"

"That's not our call, of course. I'd say that, in the end, it's probably what the Crown'll do, concede that Finger was coerced, and the other charges, auto theft and the rest, will go with it. All the sole responsibility of Louis Henderson, except for the murder of Lawrence Henderson. Reg Phelps's confession wiped out any suggestion the robbers were involved in his death."

"Tragic accident... Fuck this is going to make us look bad."

"Yeah, we're gonna look like first-class assholes for raising all the doubts about the identity of Louis that we did, and being insensitive to two women, one who said she was a kidnap victim, and the other who said she was helping her escape."

"Fuck." Wilde stood up, his anxiety inflating him. "I expect this'll be a lawsuit and a bunch of lurid headlines. Fuck!"

174

40.

I don't think it's blood money

"But I still don't want to take it if it's blood money," said Ida.

The women were back at Ida's after visiting Keith in jail. Coming home and finding the money and the note on Ida's kitchen table had taken them there.

"I don't think it's blood money, sweetie," said Sally. "You heard Keith; it didn't come from Hayes's place. Louis didn't even go to the farm."

"Poor Louis. His son... So then where did the money come from?"

"I don't know. Maybe what Keith said, that Louis took bonds or something from his brother's place. They would have gone to Louis anyway after that kid murdered Larry, so it was his own money."

"And his brother's dead too...again. Poor Louis. Two deaths of loved ones in two weeks." Ida drifted off in emotional ambivalence. She hated Louis as only a betrayed lover can hate, but her emotions had been softened by the discovery of the money. After a couple of minutes she said, "I still can't believe he left me all this money. I can understand leaving some for Keith, to help him with his lawyer costs and the like – it was Louis's son he avenged after all – but me? Louie must really love me."

Sally stifled her reaction, a soft guffaw, rolled eyes. Then, with somewhat more sympathy she recalled that Louis had, after all, shouldered the blame for the robbery, and he had left Ida a hundred grand. Maybe her friend was right about him.

"Good thing I stuck to our story," Ida said. "My lawyer said it's helping our case enormously that my story matches what Louie said, exactly, point for point, because there was no way we could have cooked it up together when I was in jail."

"So, what now?"

"Well, once these charges are behind us, I'd say we get some travel brochures."

41.

Two weeks later: America doesn't like its citizens bein' free

"It's not about guilt," said Louis to Joseph as they travelled down the I90. "Few confessions are. Mine wasn't. It was a lie. The way Catholics do it in confession."

"But don't you feel any guilt?" asked Joseph.

"All the fuckin' time. But not about robbin' the bank. They got their money back. That's not why I confessed. It was for Ida. It was about con-nec-tivity."

The two drove on in silence for a few minutes until Joseph said, looking about, "I like this camper, Louis."

"Don't forget. Call me L.L."

"Okay L.L., we're free."

"Right J.F. Having the camper should help us to not get charged for vagrancy or somethin'. Get locked up for tryin' to be free. America doesn't like its citizens bein' free. They think that free spirits who don't want houses and jobs, and who don't buy all the American Dream crap, are sick and should be locked up."

Joseph laughed delightedly.

It pleased Louis no end to see Joseph so happy.

Louis had awoken that morning and just lay there. Nothing. No one was nearby, he was certain, and he was someone who had always been acutely attuned to the metaphysics of a knife in the back. It was just a matter of time, he knew, till they came after him. But it wasn't a problem. He was used to being followed.

Inconsequential Diversions

Members of the **Inconsequential Diversions Artist Collective** create unique and experimental literary works that often combine genre fiction – marked by intellectualism about social and political subjects – with imagery and other forms of written material.

Visit
https://inconsequentialdiversions.wordpress.com/

Contact
incondive@hotmail.com

New from Inconsequential Diversions

Sirens' Island. **A. Tarrant. 978-1895166521**
A multiple murder mystery that begins with death threats against a Prince Edward Island women's art collective over their new exhibition. The show (prompted by graffiti on the artist's storefront window reading: *hell is this sirens island*) is premised on the idea that sirens are a mythical expression of men's fear of women's voices and that misogynistic myth can be rewritten.

www.ingramcontent.com/pod-product-compliance
Lightning Source LLC
Chambersburg PA
CBHW031125020426
42333CB00012B/241